WHEN SILENCE IS NO LONGER AN OPTION:

Documents Illustrating Events Organized by The Institute of African Women in Religion and Culture. March 1999 – July 2000

Edited by Elizabeth Amoah

and

Mercy Amba Oduyoye

Published for Talitha Qumi Center

Institute of African Women in Religion and Culture

Trinity Theological Seminary

Legon

SWL PRESS 2002

This Edition published 2002 by SAM-WOODE LTD.
P. O. Box AN 12719,
Accra-North, Ghana.

Sam-Woode Ltd. are publishers of educational books. The publishers also undertake publishing of academic books and journals. The works published, however, reflect the opinions of their authors and not meant to represent the official position of the publishers.

ISBN: 9988-609-83-3

Printed at SWL PRESS.

CONTENTS

PART 1

GENERAL BACKGROUND

PART III

1

GENERAL BACKGROUND
THE INAUGURAL EVENT

Introduction

Trinity Theological Seminary has in its blueprint a programme intended for the enhancement of the outreach geared towards human development. After years of consultations and a year of intensive preparation, the Institute of African Women in Religion and Culture was inaugurated.

The inauguration took place on 13th March 1999 with the theme "Empowering Women for the Third Millennium." Since then Way Forward Seminars have featured the concerns we now present.

This publication brings you an overview of the public awareness effort of the Institute by way of selected papers to illustrate the scope of deliberations, from March 1999 to July 2001.

Part I contains some papers from the Way Forward Seminars. Several of them are from Seminars that have featured Trokosi, an issue that has captured global attention. The Way Forward Seminar at Peki stimulated a follow-up on trokosi which resulted in the organization of a four day Seminar at Adidome in January 2001. This was done in collaboration with the Fetish Slaves Liberation Movement, an NGO.

In part II we have included in full, papers from the first Pan-African Conference.

The Institute's focus is public awareness that will stimulate attitudinal change and action for transformation. **Documentation is not its primary focus, but a result of research that goes into the deliberations and the presentations. We are therefore producing what researchers into culture and religion, whose focus is gender, may find useful.** Not all seminars are shaped to produce written papers but videotapes and photographs are available for all Institute events, so are bound reports of some of the major seminars.

In Part III the method and process that shape the work are described.

The methodology may be gleaned from the sample correspondence, programmes, group work and other materials located in the appendices. The ethos of the Institute has been one of a Spirituality of Plurality to ensure that people of faith become a positive influence in their communities. The membership of the Advisory Board sworn in by Rev. Prof. K.A. Dickson, President of the AACC reflects this principle.

The energy and intensity with which the Institute works is captured in "The Story of the Institute" as told by Mercy Amba Oduyoye who is the director of the Institute. In this capacity she co-ordinates the efforts of many women and men working in their own localities to offer Way Forward Seminars to bring about the desired public awareness. Below then is the speech "Empowering Women for The third Millenium" that began the day of inauguration.

From the speeches and papers delivered at the event, several issues were raised to challenge faith communities and their educational institutions on the factor of gender in their own beliefs and practices and how they shape public life.

Elizabeth Amoah

Empowering Women for the Third Millennium

Mercy Amba Oduyoye

This is a happy event and we congratulate Trinity Theological College for taking the initiative to call the faith communities of our nation to the critical question of the role of religion in public life, private life, in policy-making and in influencing the tone of our lives together.

This day is even more critical as we focus on gender-sensitivity, an aspect of community life that religion certainly influences, but to which little attention is paid. This multi-religious gathering is called so that each faith community and each person of faith might from henceforth live conscious of gender imbalances and discrimination that often make women suffer and deprive our national life of more intensive contribution of women.

We are here also to demonstrate our solidarity with Trinity Theological College as it calls attention to the gender component of our changing national culture. There is much in our indigenous cultures we think we have left behind, but which continue to hurt and limit all of us especially women. Some of these are cardinally obnoxious but others are empowering and humanizing.

There is much also that sour our relationships in our various communities. Some of these derive from gender bases that we implement without being aware of how deeply "the other" is thereby devalued. This "other" is often the woman.

This event is to get faith communities to come out and openly talk about the religious and cultural sources or ways of limiting and devaluing women, which in turn result in assumptions of male entitlements that in practice signal the debasement of womanhood.

To discuss these effectively, we have to do so from the basis of thorough research that pulls in the wisdom of all women and men both rural and urban and in whatever situation they live. We want to encourage and enable research that will then be shared generally and more importantly, result in policies and programmes for reorienting ourselves. We need to generate a reorientation of the operations of gender so that we might help change and develop healthier attitudes.

This is a time for healing. We have to take all that women's organizations have unveiled and requested, and try to respond positively to these suggested ways of transforming our gender relationships. The Institute of African Women in Religion and Culture is geared towards assisting in discovering a way out of the sterile polemics and a way forward into healthier relationships that are just and generate mutual respect and care. We want to inspire theological reflection in our African context. We want to highlight women's wisdom and women's action. We want to generate programmes that encourage reciprocity and justice, harmony and dialogue.

We would like to see faith communities harnessed to transform all cultural practices that hurt women and children and to instill in their adherents, teachings that enhance our common humanity. We would like to encourage action that will bring to a closure, religious and cultural practices that demean women and promote those that enhance the dignity of our common humanity and the worth of each individual, young or old, man or woman. We celebrate this happy event that promises healing. We pray for unity of mind and spirit and for the strength to work towards overcoming all forms of violence. With this hope we shall move from this Ebenezer into our Way Forward Seminars.

WAY FORWARD SEMINARS: Concept and Structure

The Way Forward Seminars are the continuing public education effort of the Institute. The idea is to get people of faith, women and men, groups and individuals together in a public event dealing with the concerns of women in the particular area of Ghana where the meeting is being held. Usually we have one day of public lectures, symposia and whatever will call the attention of the public to the fact that the Faith Communities and Theological Institutions care about the issues women are raising.

This is followed by a two or three-day residential workshop with about 30 people. Here papers are read on the relevant issues, with a view to finding ways of involving Faith Communities and Theological Institutions in discussing what is at stake and to recommend ways of participating in bringing about life enhancing changes.

The Opening Day is also open, that is, people of all faith communities and NGO's who share the interest in gender issues may be invited. The workshops may be multi-religious or be organized to meet the needs of specific faith communities.

The hope is that the first day will be a "media event" and then later, the workshop will produce papers for publication or for further study and analysis. Seminar organizers may cultivate the media to be present and commission someone to make a video of both the Open Day and the Workshop. Seminar organizers constitute a planning team, on which a member of the Advisory Board of the Institute serves.

Following the inauguration, seminars have been held in Cape-Coast, Ho, Kumasi, Sunyani, Bolgatanga, Abetifi, Peki, Greater Accra, Winneba and Ibadan in Nigeria. There has been a National Conference at Abokobi to review the methodology and the findings.

These events generated documentation in the form of written proceedings, photographs and Video tapes. Here we have only a few of the papers. By these Seminars we are not only undertaking public education to promote transformation of attitudes but also building up archival materials for future researchers.

Welcome and keynote addresses delivered during the public session of the seminar set the tone for the event and highlight the concerns that the people in the locality of the seminar need to deal with. To illustrate this we bring you the speech of Prof. Obeng, a member of the Advisory Board of the Institute who was the organizer of the seminar at the Cape Coast University and that of the Director of education, Ho, Ms. Aidam. The latter was delivered at the one-day seminar for young and adult women on the 23rd June 1999.

CAPE-COAST

Women, Culture and Tourism in Ghana

WELCOME ADDRESS BY PROF. OBENG

Chairperson – Mr. Kwaku Konadu (Registrar of UCC)
Quest Speaker – Professor Mercy Amba Oduyoye

Deans of Faculties, Invited Guests, Colleagues, Ladies and Gentlemen

Let me start by simply stating that it gives me great pleasure to welcome all of you to this morning's seminar. As at yesterday, I was on tenterhooks wondering how this morning's event was going to turn out. But looking around this room, I feel good about the turn out.

Let me spend some minutes to throw some light on our purpose here this morning. On 13th March 1999, the Institute of African Women in Religion and Culture was inaugurated at Trinity Theological Seminary, Legon. The aim of the Institute is to promote Women's Studies in religion and culture in our theological institutions and also create gender sensitivity in our religious bodies, our churches, our mosques, our ethnic groups – indeed the whole Ghanaian community.

The director of the institute is our Guest Speaker today. I am sure that she will tell us something more about it, but I would like to point out here that the Institute will reach out to students of departments of Universities, Seminaries and Theological Colleges in Ghana and also to our women in various religious and social groups/families, both nuclear and extended. Infact its programmes are opened to the all faith communities and the general public.

In other words, all of us gathered here this morning fall within the ambit of the activities of the Institute. Religion, be it Christian, Islam, or Traditional is meant to enhance our life, and to be life giving. But there are religious beliefs and practices that are dehumanizing, impede the progress of our women, make our women play second fiddle in the society, in our churches, or the mosques, and make our women content with their lot. St. Luke had every cause to place emphasis on women in his Gospel. Are we happy with the status of majority of women in this country?

Some of these issues may have been mentioned in some other forums before. But we want to take a fresh look at these issues again from the stand point of religion, reassess the way we have handled them before and then together resolve with renewed vigor to transform attitudes and practices for the better. To give voice to the down-trodden and to promote gender sensitivity and gender justice in religion and culture.

After the inauguration of the Institute, the plan is to hold regional seminars on Women and Religion at Kumasi, Tamale, Ho and Cape Coast. Today, those of us in Cape Coast are priviledged to have the Seminar here.

The Department of Religious Studies, UCC, a center of excellence, is proud to be associated with this project. Let me quickly add here that the Department has already put some measures in place to facilitate achieving this goal. For example, the Department has a diploma programme almost ready for consideration by the Faculty of Arts Board with courses that will create awareness on all this important theme of gender sensitivity and gender justice. A program that will serve as an outreach programme. At the B.A level, the Department is ready to introduce courses like Women in Religion, Religion and Public Life and Religion and Tourism. The contents of these courses will contribute to the aim of the Institute.

In our own fields/professions too, I am sure that each one of us can make a positive contribution to enhance the status of women and to improve gender relations. That is why we are all here. Together I am sure that we can make a difference.

Once again let me extend my warmest welcome to you. A special welcome to those of you who are visiting the University of Cape Coast for the first time. I am sure you will discover before you leave what makes us so proud of our University. A special welcome also goes to our participants from Accra and Takoradi.

Welcome, all of you. We are privileged to have you with us today.

Thank you.

"My experience as a woman public figure"

Jane M. K. Aidam

Madam Chairperson,

Rev. Ministers of Religion,

I am grateful to the organizers of this seminar, first for bringing us together as young and adult women to share our experiences in order to attempt fashioning out advancement programmes for women.

Secondly, Madam Chairperson, may I thank the organizers for extending to me a personal invitation to participate in this thought-provoking experience. To my listeners, I say welcome and ask you to lend me your ears.

It is true that as a woman public figure of the noble teaching profession, my occupation and position permit me to duly tour very remote areas normally deprived of amenities required for modest living i.e. unmotorable roads, poor or uninhabitable housing, unclean and unsafe drinking water, unhealthy environment and an ambiance of general squalor and poverty.

I have seen women building their own houses with their own hands, (providing their own shelter). I have seen women working with diseased conditions that are ravaging themselves and their children. They suffer unnoticed.

Everyday women are managing the crops, feeding and caring for their children and husbands or households, providing water and fire-wood, more or less shouldering all the responsibilities under protest.

Many women are caught up in disasters, conflict and violent situations, rendered homeless or harassed unduly.

Too many are treated as children under our laws and customs, unable to inherit their husbands' estates or even family estates, and also to secure credit of their own. They cannot find good healthy work.

Permit me to say lastly that women and the girl child are still being fed less and last and are considered for education opportunities after the last male has received his share. I must admit there is a change but it is not significant enough.

These and many more situations which I cannot mention here, have repercussions **on my life as a woman public figure**. These continue to haunt my conscience everyday as I sit in my office or in the comfort of my home. Yet I am apparently powerless as an individual, unable to meet the needs.

Madam Chairperson, permit me to express my gratitude to the 31st December Women's Movement and other progressive women organizations - not forgetting the Institute of Women in Religion and Culture who have taken it upon themselves to work together for the advancement of women.

Besides these observations, on the domestic front, I am at times caught up between and betwixt as to where the priority lies. I have children who need my tender care and attention. I have relatives, husband, in-laws etc. to manage. At the same time duty calls me to spend more and more time in the office and outside the office. Combining these responsibilities is often challenging. However, my advice is that we must carefully marry our domestic responsibilities with our official duties in a way that will maintain the status quo. Many a home has been broken arising out of this conflict of interest and pressure. As women, we have a sacred responsibility to our children and husbands. It is no different at the office. Indeed there are days when people scorn your authority just because it emanates from a woman.

There are many good situations anyway. The mere nature of a woman at times commands respect from the general public. You are treated as a "fair lady" or in colloquial terms as the weaker sex.

There are other situations where men find difficulty in taking your instructions. This is understandable at times. But where arrogance and pride come in, lines of instruction can become means of revolt which, when not contained and tolerated, can erupt and develop into enmity affecting discipline, morale, and finally hamper the process of smooth administration.

On the social front, I am proud to say that though ridiculed, women's power is often respected at social gatherings and functions such as churches, parties, and in offices such as banks and hospitals etc.

It is true that knowledge is power, power to understand issues, to fight for your rights, power to enable you seek legal counsel and attorney as and when necessary, power that keeps us informed.

Everything we do as individuals, as parents, as grandparents, as citizens, begins with our children. Giving our children the chance to learn, to grow, to dance, to sing, to become who they are meant to be, to give them the opportunity to fulfill their own dreams is our duty.

If women are empowered, respected, given the chance to live out their own dreams, then our children who depend so much on them will have full and whole lives.

And so if I look out at this crowd of distinguished women from so many walks of life, I know you share my beliefs. This is the greatest challenge to me as a public figure. How much time do I give to my children to achieve this aim.

"Where do human rights begin?" in small places, close to home, so close and so small that they cannot be seen on any map of the world, yet they are the world of the individual person. The neighborhoods we live in, the factory, farm or office, market place where we sell. Such are the places where every woman and child seeks equal justice, equal opportunity and dignity without discrimination. Unless these rights have meaning at the individual's habitat, they will have no meaning even in the highest courts - the supreme courts.

Understanding then the plight of the woman public figure at home, on the streets, in the office, factory, business, market, at the hospital, airport etc, she is faced with a life of hostility alternated with hospitality in different dimensions. It has not been easy however, it has also been welcomed.

My experiences have been at times rough; at times pleasant but in most cases challenging and rewarding.

Madam Chairperson, Distinguished Guests, Fellow Women, there is much work to be done to accord the woman public figure the equality she deserves in a world dominated by men, calling for more education for women.

Thank you and may God bless you.

2

TABLING CONCERNS

CULTURAL CONTEXT

The changing perceptives of some Akan beliefs and practices

Elizabeth Amoah

This brief presentation is part of an ongoing research on the changing perspectives of Akan traditional beliefs and practices. The Akan of Ghana is an ethnic group, which has been widely researched by eminent ethnographers such as Rattary, Busia etc. Briefly, the Akan, a multi-ethnic grouping, occupies a large sector of the southern half of Ghana. Most of the ethnic groups which constitute the Akan are basically matrilineal and this means among other things, that descent is traced through the mother's line.

The traditional culture, that is the beliefs, values, symbolic expressions, language and all the various ways of life which are typical of the Akan, has never been static. In fact, the following Akan proverb, *se mmere dane a, wo so wo dane wo ho.* , which means, when times change, you also change your way of life, would seem to suggest that the Akan cultural heritage has its own internal system which encourages change. However, there is the need to emphasize that in the course of the changes that have beset the African societies including that of the Akan, many aspects of the religious heritage, particularly the Akan traditional religious heritage, have often shown themselves to be very much alive. Two of such resilient aspects of the traditional Akan religious heritage, a heritage which puts much emphasis on the reality of a community of spirits whose powers are sought basically for ensuring life in its totality, will form the focus of this brief presentation.

But first, I would like to note here that religion, according to the traditional Akan, permeates all aspects of life and that the religious beliefs and values have impact on the meaning and interpretations given to the natural distinction between men and women. For example, the traditional Akan generally believes that each and everyone has a spiritual component *sunsum,* which protects people from the attack of all types of malevolent spirits. Women's *sunsum,* it is believed is weaker than that of the man whose *sunsum,* most invariably, is said to protect women and children who are said to be easy victims of bad spirits.

On the basis of such meaning and interpretations, which are always formulated to reflect particular needs and situation at specific times, the Akan have created clear stereotypes regarding the roles, expectations, values, and conceptions of how men and women should relate. For example, in many Akan communities some of the labels given to women are, witches, greedy, gossips and unfaithful. As such husbands are, often times, advised not to share any secrets with their wives.

Again, because women are deemed greedy, quarrelsome and to have weak *sunsum,* they are easily accused of possessing witchcraft, a malevolent spirit, according to Akan belief. At the same time, women are said to be source of life. Precisely because being a woman implies the ability to reproduce children, the Akan adolescent girls traditionally go through more elaborate puberty rituals, which are heavily loaded with symbolism of life, than the Akan boys do. On the other hand, the Akan traditional societies regard men as being brave, protective and wise so that they are expected neither to weep under any circumstances nor to be insulted as being fools or unwise. As such, many men set themselves very high ideals and goals. When such ideals and goals are unfulfilled, they accuse their mothers and grandmothers who have nurtured them through their lives, for impeding their progress with witchcraft. Men never blame themselves for their failures.

The point I am trying to make is that these cultural or human-made interpretations and meanings give rise to the differing images of men and women in the society which, from birth to death, train and treat people according to the labels male and female. It is important to note here however, that these categories and labels are not peculiar to the Akan. Among human beings, as with plants and animals, there are males and females. The Akan for example, will not sell his or her hen unnecessarily, the rationale being that the hen will produce more fowls. Male fowls and cattle are more dispensable.

In the Akan traditional religious systems too, women's full participation in the religious activities is greatly affected by the meaning and the interpretations given to their biological and natural functions. For example, the natural process of menstruation which normally women go through at some stage of life, has ambiguously been interpreted by many Akan communities as powerful, potent, polluting and dirty. It is on the basis of this for example, that we can explain why in some religious activities women are excluded or preferred. In the purification rituals of Akan stool rooms, menopausal women (who are seen as transformed into men with the cessation of menstruation) are preferred to menstruating women precisely because the menstrual blood, as perceived by the traditional Akan, weakens the potency of the ancestors or any religious objects. Hence, menstruating women who have religious functions are expected to curtail their religious roles at such times.

What bothers my mind is the obsessed fear of menstruation, for in the Akan traditional communities the menstrual blood signifies the ability to give life. Hence, the onset of it is heralded amidst elaborate ritual celebration, *bragoro,* which means, the celebration of life. The issue then is, if menstruation is a symbol of life, why is it said to be dirty and polluting? Is this an attempt to control the ritual power of women, one may ask? Obviously, this to me, is a clear case of ambiguity arising from the religio-cultural perception of women.

Another aspect of Akan traditional religion in which a clear case of ambiguous perception of women is obvious is that of witchcraft and witchcraft accusation. My intention here is not to argue whether witchcraft exists or not. For, like any other religious belief and experience, it will be futile to accurately verify through empirical means. One thing, which echoes in my ear though, is what my grandmother kept on saying to me- "It is the witch who sees the fellow witch." My concern here is with those accused of witchcraft, a craft which is basically seen as deadly, destructive and evil. Why is it that women, mothers-in law, relatives and grand- mothers of those who do not make it in life, and these days, house- helpers, particularly young girls are often accused of the destructive and evil craft? Who are accusing these women of witchcraft? Under what circumstances do women confess being witches? Why should witchcraft be necessarily evil? These and similar issues need to focus our attention in the search for a renewed community in which both men and women feel comfortable with each other.

Again, is it not ambiguous and strange that many women who are generally stereotyped as peace loving, as good parents who work around the clock to nurture people, are labeled as witches at some point in their lives? Or, women who give and nurture life are said to destroy the same life that they give? Of course men have witchcraft but as usual, theirs is said to be more potent and positive than that of the women.

Witchcraft accusation is one of the several ways by which the Akan society inflicts all types of violence against women. Surely, no woman who is accused of witchcraft will be given the opportunity to realize her full potential in religion or society. The experiences that she goes through as a witch, a social deviant, is so traumatic and violent that she is almost invariably hastened to her grave or pushed to the periphery forever. Obviously there is something more to the witchcraft phenomenon as perceived in the Akan society than just being an evil power, which possesses women. In my view, witchcraft is a neutral spirit that is assigned moral values when it gets into people. Otherwise, it is difficult to explain how a basically evil spirit becomes a good spirit when it gets into men, for example. Or, is this another way of controlling women's abilities as it is portrayed in the following Akan cultural statements, which condition actions and attitudes?

1) *Akoko bere so nim adekyee nso ohwɛ onin ano* (Christaller)
   This means, the hen too knows when it is dawn. However, it looks up to the cock to announce it.
2) *Obaa ton nyadowa na onntone atuduro* (Christaller)
   A woman sells garden eggs and not gunpowder.
3) *Se obea tɔ tuo a, esi beema dan mu.* (Christaller)

If a woman buys a gun, she keeps it in a man's room.

My interpretation and meaning to them are the following. The first proverb, which indicates the gender slant of societal roles, implies that traditionally, the potential of women should be sacrificed so that men can realize their potential. Sadly enough, some women do not appreciate the irrelevance of this cultural statement, particularly when these days, there are, symbolically speaking, some women who are not leaving "crowing to the cocks." My own Hall, Volta Hall for instance, still has the symbol of the proud hen allowing the cock to crow on the Hall's crest.

The second proverb illustrates how the roles in the society have a gender bias. That is, there are specific roles for men and women and that these roles should not be crossed over. Currently with the rapid and changing situations, this strict division of roles in the economic sphere as implied in the above proverb seems to be irrelevant, particularly when the economic activities of some women in Ghana these days include the sale of ammunition, a venture which was preserved for men. Similarly, some men have also crossed over to economic activities such as the sale of cooked food, traditionally a prerogative of Ghanaian women. After the exodus of the Ghanaians from Nigeria in the eighties, many men, Akan men included, went into the 'Chop bar' industry, for example. In other words, in the context of the Ghanaian changing situations, the Akan cultural emphasis on strict division of labor does not necessarily hold for some Ghanaians.

Again, the third proverb, which alludes to the fact that women's guns are eventually kept in the men's room clearly implies the control of men over the activities of women, even in the domestic sphere, not withstanding the wide range of interpretation of the Akan word for gun, e*tuo*.

In my opinion, the main thrust of some Akan religious beliefs and cultural statements is that role and expectations and perceptions are clearly gender based and that in some instances, men have control over certain vital activities of women. Thus, in a way, the Akan cultural heritage gives men the opportunity and power to control women. However, as situations inevitably change so do the cultural perceptions and interpretations that have been given to the natural distinctions between men and women change. Thus, these cultural stereotypes such as, men do not weep, women cannot be trusted as the traditional Akan believe, should not be seen as static. As was said earlier on in this paper, the Akan cultural heritage is not against change. It is becoming very unfashionable to hold unto cultural stereotypes which are losing fast their essence and relevance. Again, the Akan tradition reminds us that when times change, you also change. Cultural beliefs and practices including religious meaning and interpretations have never remained the same. What people do and say day-to-day with regard to what goes on around them, to some extent, contribute to the various processes of change which is inevitable in every culture. This Institute of Women in Religion and Culture, which is inaugurated today is part of the processes of change and therefore needs to be supported.

A CHURCH WOMAN
Overcoming violence against women

Theresa Acolatse

Women of faith who are we? As I travel participating in church and social activities, this question is of great concern to women of all denominations, creed and color. Consequently, as we journey into the new millennium with Bible Study, and women's concerns to be addressed, it is imperative that we assess the status of women in our churches. This assessment will give greater appreciation, understanding and a positive mind-set as we minister to others. Looking at our past and present will give us a handle on how we view ourselves as "a person". The better we feel about ourselves, the more effective and genuine our ministry can be to others. Moreover, this view will help us to get a glimpse of the future status of women as useful and valued part of the Body of Christ. Thus a look at the evolution of the classical role of women in the church is essential.

Nearly two thousand years ago, the first Christian Communities came into existence. During these years, the church structure grew and developed into many channels through which its activities were conducted. Men have led the activities predominantly. However, during this present century, significant changes have occurred. People have become more aware of all forms of oppression and discrimination especially as they relate to women. In recent years, there has been a growing awareness of oppression and discrimination against women who have been deprived of honor and recognition in leadership position. Now because of historical and spiritual reasons, male dominance in church leadership is being challenged and replaced with a church structure that gives equal honor and opportunity to both sexes.

Three dimensional perspectives of women in the church

- Research has revealed that in general from a historical perspective the lot of women in the church has been bleak. The deplorable status and treatment of women are observed by many. Nearly 2000 years ago, the first institutionalized Christian Churches came into existence and since their inception, women have been deprived of honor and recognition in leadership positions. Various reasons have been found. Commentaries suggest that one of the reasons of conflicting viewpoints among Christians, is a result of inaccurate knowledge of the text and the lack of acquaintance with the culture of the time in which the Bible was written. Secondly it is commonly assumed that Jesus chose twelve men to be His inner circle of disciples, and had no place in His entourage for women. However, the gospel indicates that women did travel with Jesus, many of them - some were married and others were single (Luke 8:1-3). Women were often recipients of his teachings (Matt.15: 38). Moreover in the Garden of Eden, God blessed **both** Adam and Eve with five blessing:

Be **Fruitful** and **Multiply**
and **Replenish** the earth
and **subdue** it
and have **Dominion**....... (Gen.1: 28).

Now I can say for myself that I really face up to the great degree of partiality that exists in the organized church of this world. In some churches, women are forbidden to hold any offices other than in some auxiliaries or clubs such as The Hostess Club, Pastor's Aide or Mothers' Club. But it was obvious from my search of the scriptures that God's plan included all who are saved by His Grace for He gives us the gifts He wants us to use in serving Him. Surely, as perfect and fair as God is, He has given women spiritual gifts that would carry us beyond the ranks of the pastor's aide club, etc. Our spiritual gifts are no different from those given to men for they are from the same source (I Cor. 4). This institutional sexism is violence against women.

Given the cultural background of the first century Palestine, Jesus showed a remarkable sensitivity to women; He had respect for their ability to grasp and understand spiritual truths and He considered them worthy recipients of some of His most profound teaching. To overcome violence against women we need the example of Jesus and of men, who like Him, saw and dealt with women as human beings and children of God.

Current situations of women in the A.M.E. Zion Church

In the U.S.A many women worked by the side of their husbands and fathers in establishing the AME Zion Church in 1796, though they held no leadership roles and were silent participants in the life of the church. I salute those pioneering women. Those were the pillars that enabled Zion to build the many serviceable churches in the world today.

When progress had to be made, the women were willing to sacrifice and toil.

They proved to be towers of strength to the courageous men of Zion. Now we see women of Zion serving and working out "their soul salvation" at almost every level of the church. In some arenas, they are more accepted than others, however, in others they have not yet been admitted. Nevertheless, our present memories of the hot issues of the 80s and 90s make us realize that the church has been a priority item in women's reflections. We have learnt a new identity for females as a whole. Today, women are not sitting back and shutting up despite the obstacles put in their way. In all walks of life the message is clear. ***"Women are people of worth and dignity".*** They are not to be placed in sub-human roles or looked down upon. Therefore, it is during our present era, that Philippians 4:13 becomes more apparent to the women of the Church, it states, **"I *can do all things through Christ who strengthens me".***

The emerging new model of women in the church

The emerging model of progressive women in the church will have to be intertwined with the past and present memories that will bring new hope for us all. Consequently, according to Swidoll, a balanced woman of God will emerge and have the following traits:

- A balanced woman of God sees Scripture as God's vital relevant Word worth her attention, devotion and application (see the story of Timothy's mother 2 Tim. 1:3-5)

- A balanced woman of God sees herself **valuable, gifted, responsible for her own growth** and **maturity** ... not overly dependent on anyone to get her through life or to make her secure (Acts 16:11-15).

- A balanced woman of God sees the Lord as her **strength,** her **refuge** and her **shield** when things refuse to be resolved (Acts 21:7-14).

The challenge to all women is to work and eliminate the personal and institutional sexism in our local churches and denominations as well as in the community. Christian Women, the world over, have a special birthright to claim and protect. Esau treated his birthright lightly and finally he sold it for red pottage. Women can sell their spiritual birthright also by feeling that their only place is the kitchen. We can be good cooks and should be but we do not have a monopoly of this skill. We also have a divine heritage to minister in our own unique situations, and none can do that for us. Go forth and serve where God intends you to serve. Let us be committed to changing the secondary role played by women in the church so that both women and the church can continue to progress.

ORDAINED WOMAN
Women who influenced religion

Eunice S. A. Kpikpi

I am grateful to the Almighty Father for giving me the opportunity to dilate on the topic 'Women who influenced Religion".

God in His own wisdom has created both man and woman in His own image (Gen. 1:26-17). Therefore masculinity and feminity must both be in His nature. But all along in history women had been marginalized, oppressed, and exploited morally, socially, economically, and religiously. The Bible which is the word of God to all humankind is male oriented and injunctions are put here and there on women as to what they may or may not do in the Lord's vineyard (I Cor. 14:34-3, 1 Tim. 2:115).

But as the years have passed by women have found their traditional roles as defined by men unrealistic and frustrating. New ideas are spreading in society, emphasizing the basic equality and human rights for all people. There are new winds blowing across the Christian world. Women have become bold and are trying to identify God's image in them as equal human beings who just like men have been put in the Lord's Vineyard to work and take care of it.We are grateful to God that some men have got this awareness and are encouraging women to fight the good fight to the end. We thank these our noble brothers who are giving us the moral support. Your efforts will not be in vain. Turning to our topic "Women who influenced Religion" I would like to recall some biblical women who brought salvation to their people.

- Sarah, despite her old age became the mother of the great nation God promised Abraham (Gen. 21:1-7).
- Moses who became the great leader of the Israelites was saved by God through the hands of noble women He had set aside
- The Egyptian midwives, Shiphrah and Puah who defied Pharaoh's authority by not killing baby Moses. (Exo. 1: 15)
- The mother of Moses who hid him in the river Nile
- The Sister of Moses, Miriam, who kept watch over the baby and brought Moses' own mother to breast-feed him.
- Pharaoh's daughter who adopted Moses
- Zipporah, Moses' wife, who saved his life when God had wanted to kill Moses on his way back to Egypt. Moses (Ex. 4:24)

All the above-named women saved the life of Moses who became the founder of Yahwestic Religion.

- Miriam, the sister of Moses, again was made a prophetess accompanying her brothers Moses and Aaron (Mich. 6-4) who led the Israelites to the land of Canaan.
- Naomi and Ruth were the great **ancestresses** of the Davidic dynasty and feature in Jesus' birth lineage.
- Rahab, the harlot, saved the lives of the two spies Joshua sent to Jericho.
- Deborah was a judge and a prophetess. She led the army that destroyed the Canaanite Army and their Commander Sisera (Judges 4;1)
- Esther's wisdom saved the Jewish religion and Community in the Persian **Empire. (The book of Esther)**

Just as God made use of women to bring salvation to human-kind in the Old Testament, He made use of women in the New Testament as well.

- Mary, the mother of Jesus, it was through her the whole world has got salvation (Luke 1;42)
- Anna, the prophetess (the daughter of Phanuel (Luke. 2:36)
- The 4 daughters of Phillip who were prophetesses (Acts. 21: 8-9)
- Pricilla assisted her husband in teaching (Acts. 18:24-26) and proclaiming the Gospel.
- In Roman chap. 16, Paul mentioned Phoebe and Junia who were apostles. He also mentioned Tryphena and **Tryphosa** who were also women. In Phil 4:2-3 **Euodias** and Synthche (women) were leaders in the Church in Philippi.

  Indeed, before God "there is neither Jew nor Greek, there is neither bond nor free, there is neither male nor female, for ye are all one in Christ Jesus". (Gal. 3:28) God is no respecter of persons (Act 10:34).

  Just as we have women who influenced religion positively, so do we have some who had negative influence on it, women like Solomon's wives who were Moabites, Ammonites, Edommites,

Zidonians and Hittittes. These wives turned Solomon's heart after other gods and his heart was not devoted to his God. (1 Kings 11:6)

Samson's wife Delilah, a prostitute who betrayed him to the Philistines that caused him his death (Judge chapter 16)

Jezebel's influence on her husband to kill Naboth because of his own vineyard.

Hebrew women who encouraged their dishonest men (husbands) to cheat the poor and the needy. (Amos chapter 4) and many more.

But the question is, do we as women, created in the Image of God influence religion positively or negatively? Since religion is a way of life, let us re-examine our calling - i.e. our priesthood together under the cross with men towards the next millennium

My question to all of us is how are we influencing religion in our communities to bring salvation and liberation to those who are being oppressed like the Trokosi system we have just talked of?

TRADITIONAL RULER (A MAN)
The role of women in the Ghanaian culture.

Togbega Garusu VI

To be able to do justice to the topic, there is the need to dilate briefly on what culture is. While a school child in Ghana may explain culture as drumming, singing, and dancing and also acting of plays, because these are the aspects of culture the innocent child has been consciously exposed to, the more read scholars and their contemporaries would say that culture is the totality of the way of life of a people.

If we all accept what the scholars say culture is, then I crave your indulgence to recast my topic as - the role of women in the Ghanaian way of life.

Chairperson, Ghanaians like all other peoples of the world have a unique way of life which not only differentiates them from, but also harmonizes them with the rest of the world.

Ghanaian men and women have their respective roles- roles which identify them sex by sex, but at the same time bring them together as Ghanaians for the task of family and nation building. In all this, the role of the Ghanaian women stands out conspicuously in the daily activities of the family and the nation as a whole.

As culture is dynamic, some of the roles Ghanaian women used to play have given way to new ones or just died off according to the dynamics of culture.

In view of time limitations ... Chairman, I shall like to dwell on just a few aspects of the Ghanaian way of life and the roles our women play in it. The areas of concentration are Birth, Sickness/Death, Education, Religion /Politics, Land/Agriculture/food, Chieftaincy.

In the human race it is women who carry and give birth to babies. Seriously speaking, many of us here might not be carrying the names we proudly get along with if our mothers had decided that it was the other man, and not our father who was responsible for the pregnancy. From this it is at once clear that women, Ghanaian women included, play a very crucial role in deciding parentage.

After the child is born, the Ghanaian woman doubles for mother and nurse, and even as a teacher, bringing up the child to the best of her ability. It is in this way all the great men and women we often hear talked about were brought up. It is because of this type of up-bringing from our mothers that Ghanaians enjoy so much peace now.

It is when the so-called modern Ghanaian women started shirking the responsibility of motherhood by leaving their babies with caretakers, feeding the baby on processed food that our youth began to behave like the animals whose milk they fed on as babies. Government policies need to assist women to play their proper roles as mothers.

Sickness/Death:

In Ghana, the responsibility for caring for the sick is mostly for women. The best the man does is to supply the funds. The core part of the care-feeding, washing, removing the pail and others is completely left on the woman.

Also in the case of death, the very important rites like washing the corpse, and in some circumstances preserving the corpse till burial, where there is no mortuary, laying in state and watching over the corpse are all for the women, at times at great risks to their health.

Religion/Medicine

In the Ghanaian traditional set up, women play just as important roles as their male counterparts. Many women are heads of religious groups where they play the role of priestesses and also the role of healers.

Religious groups headed by women are found to last longer than those headed by men. You may want to research this assertion. Despite this success story of women religious leaders, Christian churches are reluctant to give our women the right to serve at the higher levels of their hierarchy.

It is time these Christian churches remembered that Christianity would have ended with the crucifixion and death of Jesus but for the women who followed Jesus to the very end. Women (Mary and others) had to venture out to find out how the body of Jesus fared in the tomb, while the apostles (men) locked themselves up, afraid to come out to avoid persecution.

It is time Ghana sets foot on the right by accepting women at all levels of our Christian religious practices.

Politics

Until very recently, the Ghanaian woman was not encouraged to do politics. It was considered dirty, reserved for men who were crooks, and of course women who were prostitutes, etc.

Thanks to the 31st December Women's Movement, this situation has changed and the Ghanaian woman has found her tongue. Politics in Ghana has been cleansed, making it wholesome for women to be involved in it. It is however necessary to encourage women further. We still have to persuade some husbands to desist from forbidding their wives from accepting high positions in government.

Also sexual harassment should be seriously dealt with so women who are generally upright would not fear to rub shoulders with their men counterparts, in politics and in the work place.

Education:

The famous Ghanaian Educator, Kwegyir Aggrey, had said long ago, "Educate a woman and you educate a nation. Educate a man and educate an individual". In spite of this being on all lips education is one area where the Ghanaian women had been side-lined until recently. The saying was " the place of the women was the kitchen" and our school reading books confirmed this with sentences like, "Kofi is reading a book, and Ama is pounding fufu."

With the realization that the education of a woman is even more beneficial than that of a man, the situation has changed, and this change of the situation has positively reflected in better care for our children, better care for our sick, and in fact a better outlook for our families."

Land/Agriculture/Food.

Among some Ghanaian ethnic groups, women do not hold the ownership or title deeds to land especially when the land belongs to another family. This is because it was feared that the title might get into the wrong hand as a result of the women's marriage into another family.

On the other hand it has been noted that women produce the bulk of the food we live on, and food is produced on land. This brings into question whether the Ghanaian women who make the most use of the land should be denied ownership of land.

Ghana is not an industrial country and cannot boast of many big food processing plants. The processing and preservation of especially the local staples is done by women, who depend on the age-old traditional methods handed down from their mothers.

Again, marketing of the food items is done mostly by the women who travel all over the country for these purposes. To enable the Ghanaian women to play their role in the production, processing and marketing of their produce, there is the need to introduce them to the appropriate training schemes to enhance their efforts.

Chieftaincy

Chieftaincy is one of the oldest institutions in Ghana. It is the brewing pot for all our culture. It is around this institution that our culture is hinged. Chieftaincy is the institution that holds Ghana together, considering the fact that governments are so to say, **very** remote from the people. Surprisingly the role of the "Ghanaian women in this sacred institution is the most paramount. For almost all the ethnic groups in Ghana except may be, those in the north of Ghana, the onus or responsibility for the choice of a good chief lies on women i.e. the Queen mother. A typical example is the Asante, and this was vividly demonstrated in the recent selection of the current Asantehene in the person of Otumfuo Nana Osei Tutu II.

It is not only the selection of the Chief that behoves the Queen Mother. In many cases before even the chief declares war he must consult the Queen mother. In time of war, it is the Queen mother who decides where the ancestral stool should be kept to prevent enemies from capturing it.

The above responsibilities of the Queen mother require some sterling qualities, such as wisdom, courage, truthfulness and faithfulness and these are qualities-found in almost all Ghanaian women.

Chairperson, Ladies and Gentlemen,

I have, for these few minutes, tried to bring into focus some of the roles Ghanaian women play or are expected to play as their contribution towards the development of the nation.

It is our responsibility as citizens of Ghana, both individually and collectively, to assist in enhancing the roles of Ghanaian women for better results.

3

FOCUS ON TROKOSI

"What Is Trokosi System?"

Mark Wisdom

Mr. Chairman, Ladies and Gentlemen, first of all, let us examine closely the etymology of the name TROKOSI. The people of Tongu call it TROKOSI. TRO means deity. Kosi means female slave. Hence TRO-KOSI means female slave of a deity. KLUVI, means male slave. The people of Anlo call it FIASIDI. FIASI means priest of a deity.

DI means wife or woman that can only be married to a Priest. Therefore, FIASI-DI simply means fetish priest's wife. (With the disparaging remarks about African Religion that came with Westernization and Christianity **fiasi** has also come to mean "a charlatan")

In the Ada language, the real name is YO-NYORGUE which is turned into YO-KUE. YO means woman NYORGUE means slave.

Therefore, YO-KUE also simply means female slave. The Tongu, Anlo and Ada ethnic groups or communities practise the Tro-kosi system. That is to say, Trokosi system is practised in the North Tongu, South Tongu, Akatsi, Ketu, Keta, East Dangbe and West Dangbe Districts.

Trokosi is an ancient, traditional and cruel practice or cult whose custom demands that only girls or women should atone for offences or crimes committed by any member of the family. The custom also demands that generations should continue paying for one and the same offence. In other words, when a slave or Trokosi dies, there should be a replacement from the same family and also for the same offence and this must go on *ad infinitum*. Girls aged between 5 and 20 years are accepted in the shrine. Those who reach the age of puberty are raped by the priests soon after. The younger ones have to wait for their turn.They are consequently forced to marry the priests against their will.

This heinous custom demands that the parents of the Trokosi should look after them and their children. That is, their parents should send food from time to time to the slaves in the shrine. These slaves should be given parcels of land to cultivate food crops to supplement what they receive from their parents. The Trokosi cult also stresses that the Priests should have no domestic responsibility whatsoever towards the slave. Even if they are hungry the Priests should not give them food to eat. As a result of this, sometimes the slaves starve in the shrine.

They are also seriously malnourished. There are no doors to their rooms in order to give easy access to the Priests for sexual satisfaction whenever they feel like it. They are either beaten mercilessly by the Priests at the slightest provocation, or made to pay a fine ranging from money to a goat or sheep. One can therefore find them in the bush cutting or looking for firewood to sell so as to pay such fines. Their sufferings or burdens are compounded by all this. And yet they have no alternative but to obey or dance to the tune at the Priests' command because they are paying for a crime.

The Trokosi are obliged to work on the Priests' farm all day without rest. They have no right to come home before sunset. They work in the sun with their babies at their back. While other children belonging to them are also in the bush crying. They leave home for the farm before sunrise.

This horrible custom stresses further that the slaves should not consume any food crops harvested from the Priests' farm. The Priests can use as much food as they can, and sell the rest. But none whatsoever should be given to the Trokosi; otherwise it amounts to violating the custom which stipulates that the Priests should not look after them.

At this juncture I wish to state categorically that it is very wicked of those who say that the Trokosi girls are not slaves or do not suffer in the shrines.

What are the offences or crimes which demand this perpetual punishment or suffering?

Stealing some money, say, five thousand cedis, a goat or even a fowl; accusing someone of something, which he or she has not done. The victim becomes alarmed and evokes a deity to intervene. The victim goes to consult the particular deity he or she has evoked.

Mysteriously, people begin to die in the culprit's family, one after the other at short intervals, to the extent that the family becomes panic-stricken and consults a soothsayer who readily tells them why people are dying at short intervals in the family. Then the soothsayer advises the family to see the particular Priest in charge of that shrine. The Priest in turn confirms the cause of the successive deaths within a short space of time in the family, and requests for a young girl to be brought to the shrine to pacify the deities. As soon as a girl is sent to the shrine, the mysterious deaths cease.

All Trokosi girls are initiated into the Trokosi cult. At the initiation, a Priest will hide himself in a dark room, at the time the girls would be told that as wives of the deities, they have to go into that dark room and meet their spiritual husband. As soon as the girl enters the room, the Priest would hold her firmly and have sex with her. After this shameful act, each girl is given a small box containing some evil spiritual powers to keep.

Parents would discuss secretly behind closed doors which of their daughters to send to the shrine. The parents then ask the girl to accompany them to see someone in a village unknown to the girl. Meanwhile, a message is sent to the Priest to expect them. At the village, she sees this strange man for the first time. During discussion the parents would introduce their daughter to the Priest secretly and pretend to greet someone nearby, while they ask the young innocent girl to wait for them. The parents would dodge the girl and double up their steps home, leaving the girl behind. The poor unsuspecting girl would wait and wait for hours in vain for her parents. By the time she realizes that she has been deceived and abandoned by her parents, she would burst into uncontrollable tears and cry all day and night.

Some of the Trokosi told us that they nearly committed suicide when this happened to them. Others said they refused to eat for days. They were horrified when the Priest approached them at night to have sex with them. They wept bitterly cursing their parents who brought them to the shrine. They felt homesick of their parents, brothers and sisters and their classmates. Let us remember that most of these Trokosi were withdrawn from school and their education for that matter curtailed.

Trokosi system prevents girls from going to school, it imprisons talents; it is, in fact, one of the main causes of illiteracy, ignorance, poverty and backwardness among women in some communities in Ghana.

The Trokosi system is in flagrant violation of human rights or women's rights. It favours torture and cruelty; it is an outmoded custom, which should cease to exist as soon as possible. It must be eradicated entirely from the Ghanaian society.

Generally, Trokosi are supposed to spend their entire lives in the shrine. But if she becomes less attractive physically owing to suffering, emotional stress, malnutrition, starvation and hard work, the Priest may allow her to stay henceforth outside the shrine and even get married to another man, pending a replacement at her death. This is what we call FIA in Ewe. However, if their Priest dies and another is installed, the custom demands that all those staying outside the shrine should go back to the shrine and have sex with the new Priest for three months before going back, even if they are married to someone else outside the shrine, The new husband has no alternative but to wait while his wife goes back to the shrine to fulfill the demand of this custom. This custom is called FIADOMENYINU in Ewe. Isn't this most immoral and abominable? This is most dehumanizing and a degradation of womanhood. Regarding shrine festivals, every Trokosi whether in the shrine or living outside the shrine, as explained earlier is compelled to attend. All sorts of inexplicable immoral attitudes towards the fetish slaves take place. All children born to the second husband outside the shrine belong to the Priest and must also bear his name, even though the fetish priests do not look after them.

The Campaign

As regards the historical background of the anti-Trokosi campaign, which started in 1980, I wish to explain here clearly that it wasn't my own initiative, but it was due to a vision I saw in 1977 and I would like to narrate it later. It took me some time to understand the vision. It also took me almost three years to research into the Trokosi practice after I had got to know that the vision was about Trokosi, Yewhe, Agbosu and Korku cults. Before I started the campaign I realized that everyone was afraid to either raise his voice against this cruel traditional custom or even mention it in public, for fear of being killed by the shrine powers. It was true that some few people wrote secretly reporting the Trokosi system to the colonial government, or criticized it in family circles behind closed doors. But all this could be described as bedroom politics.

To set the records straight, it was I, Mark Wisdom, who started the whole anti-Trokosi campaign in 1980, after I had investigated thoroughly this heinous traditional practice. I must say frankly here that if I were not an Ewe or a citizen of Tongu and from the same community that practises the cult, or someone whose relatives were Trokosi practitioners, I would have failed in my investigations into the practice. Later, I met with the Paramount Chief of the Mafi Traditional area, the late Togbe Asem III and explained my intention of campaigning against the Trokosi system. He was astonished and conceded that he was afraid of it himself, but he would lend me his moral support, because it was his earnest wish to liberate the Trokosi inmates. "That is very courageous of you, Mark", he said. He also helped me a lot in my investigations.

In 1982, we organized the first ever Trokosi abolition meeting at Adidome which was attended by a whole lot of Priests, shrine owners, opinion leaders, pastors, school teachers, drivers and, in fact, people of all walks of life. People from the North and South Tongu Districts and Akatsi District, including students from the Akatsi Training College attended this meeting. It was the largest gathering ever witnessed at Adidome, people remarked. At this historic meeting, presided over by the late Togbe Asem 111, I was introduced to the audience by Mr. Moses Goku, the State Secretary of Mafi Traditional Council. During his introductory statement, Mr. Goku told the gathering that 1, Mark Wisdom, invited all of them and that the Paramount Chief presiding over the meeting and he, Moses Goku, did not know what it was all about. He said this for obvious reasons.

Then I stood up to address the crowd. I spoke boldly and clearly to the audience explaining how cruel and heinous the Trokosi practice is and the need to free all the Trokosi slaves. There was a loud applause at the end of my speech, then they all shouted in one voice, "Let us abolish the Trokosi system and free the girls!" I asked them to repeat that statement three times, which they did. 1, therefore, asked them what they requested from me so as to free the slaves.

The Priests who were present quickly put their heads together and said I should bring a bottle of schnapps for libation so as to declare the slaves freed once and for all. Minutes later, someone brought me a bottle of schnapps which I handed over to the Chairman. But just at the moment Togbe Asem stood up to ask one of the Priests for the libation, one Mr. Kwame Owusu, a shrine owner from Mafi Dugame, stood up to object to the libation on that day, saying, it was too early yet, "It should be postponed for two weeks and if you, Mark Wisdom, were alive up to that time, the libation would take place and the inmates accordingly liberated", he said. I stood up to object to the idea of postponing the libation and argued it out with him in vain. So someone advised me to agree to his conditions, which I did for the sake of bringing the meeting to a civil close.

Before the stipulated two weeks elapsed, one Mr. Atsu Fevlo wrote to advise the Trokosi practitioners to refuse to release the girls. A copy of this letter was sent to Togbe Asem III who in turn served me with a copy through his Secretary, Mr. Moses Goku. Consequently, the Trokosi practitioners did not turn up for the follow-up meeting although others did.

I therefore, forwarded the case to the national level by writing a letter to the then Chairman of the P.N.D.C., Flt. Lt. J. J. Rawlings, who requested the

Minister of Culture and Tourism, Mr. Asiedu Yirenkyi and the Minister of Information, Mr. Totobi Kwakye to organise a press conference for me to address the nation. This I did and I was later attached to the Ministry of Culture and Tourism with access to the state media where I spoke on the Radio and Television for two years and I was also given a special column in the Daily Graphic where I was contributing articles regularly, educating the whole nation on the need to free the Trokosi girls. The Minister of Culture and Tourism, Mr. Asiedu Yirenkyi drew up a special programme whereby University Professors were invited to exchange ideas with me in his presence. I also discussed cultural issues with Dr. Kwabena Damuah at the request of the government.

At the end of the second year at the Ministry of Culture and Tourism, I came back to Adidome to continue visiting shrines. After ten years, two other human rights organizations, namely, Missions International and International Needs joined the struggle to free the Trokosi slaves and rehabilitate them.

One day, I visited one of the Priests' by name Togbe Aklidokpo of Avakpedome shrine and at this time, I preached the Gospel of Christ to him. He was so moved and said, "why not come to the shrine to preach to my Trokosi girls because they were too quarrelsome; and if they get converted to Christianity, I would drive them all out of the shrine". I was very happy to hear this, so the next day I went to the shrine with a team of Christian brothers and sisters. To our surprise, before we reached there the girls were made to arrange seats where inmates, the Priest, Togbe Aklidokpo and the shrine owners were all seated anxiously expecting us. In fact, allowing Christians to enter a shrine and preach the Gospel of Christ to traditionalists is unprecedented. Many people from the Avakpedome township rushed to watch what was going on. At the end of the sermon, all the Trokosi girls in the shrine gave their lives to Christ and asked to be baptized. We went there several times after that to conduct church service for them.

Later, I implored Togbe Aklidokpo to allow them to come to Adidome for literacy classes and also to apprentice them to sewing. He agreed and the Trokosi girls were attending literacy classes at my house and were also learning sewing at Madam Odzoko's workshop. I was also teaching them the modern method of farming in my garden. This was the first Trokosi Vocational School at Adidome, which was a joint venture of Missions International and Fetish Slaves Liberation Movement (FESLIM), of which I am the Executive Director.

After some time, I was invited by the First Baptist Church at Tema to give a talk on Trokosi. Togbe Aklidokpo, the Priest of Avakpedome and Madam Sharon Titiane, the Director of Missions international accompanied me. After my address, the Trokosi Vocational School was given ten sewing machines by the Tema First Baptist Church.

Later, Missions International and FESLIM entrusted the day-to-day running of the Trokosi vocational school to International Needs whose Executive Director is the Reverend Walter Pimpong.

FESLIM later conducted a general survey of the Trokosi system and discovered seven districts practising the cult as stated earlier on. Thereafter, FESLIM embarked on education by way of seminars designed to debate possible strategies for creating awareness and sensitizing the practitioners to allow us to liberate the fetish slaves whose plight was "inexplicably miserable". 'The seminars took us throughout the seven districts. The practitioners, as a result, began to see eye to eye with us which brought us now to the liberation stage.

International Needs and FESLIM have so far liberated about 2,500 Trokosi slaves. We are still left with a whole lot of them to liberate. As a matter of fact, FESLIM could have liberated all the Trokosi girls from the shrines by now, but for financial constraints. Therefore, if the Church and the society could contribute towards the liberation and rehabilitation of the Trokosi victims, we could eradicate the Trokosi system entirely in about two years.

In addition to the eradication of the Trokosi system, we have great need to liberate and rehabilitate other slaves in the other shrines, such as, Yewhe, Agbosu and Korku. These three cults are more cruel and more dehumanizing than the Trokosi system. FESLIM intends to expose them to the whole nation in due course as it has done to the Trokosi system.

The Vision

This short account will not be complete until I narrate briefly the vision that I saw concerning the liberation of these poor and unfortunate girls. One day, in a dream, I saw that I was walking on a bush path to an unknown destination when all of a sudden I came to a mighty building which looked like a law court with a mighty crowd standing in front of the building complaining of the cruelty and torture meted out to them by someone. This was after I had passed by a police station. It appeared there was someone in the room listening to them. I saw that the people looked very sad so I stopped to listen to what they were saying. One woman said, "He bruised my arm". Another said, "It is he who hurt my neck". Another woman added, "This same man has been torturing and maltreating me all my life, and I wish I were not born into this wicked world". Similar complaints were made by several other men and women in the crowd.

Suddenly a mighty deep voice thundered from the room, "Go and bring this man!" There was dead silence for some seconds. Then I saw two men come out of the crowd and began to walk away. About an hour later, a very tall giant, looking extremely strong and terrible, flanked by the two men sent after him, appeared in the distance. The whole crowd in one voice shouted, "Yes! That's the man we are talking about. He is very cruel to us". The voice in the room thundered once more, which echoed to the ceiling and shook the ceiling, saying, "Listen, you have been torturing these people from time immemorial; you shall be imprisoned". Looking very furious and annoyed, the strong man rather mysteriously stretched forth his arms which reached to the end of the crowd and pushed all of them into the small cell and locked them up. I was left by myself.

I was horrified and watched the man very closely. I have never seen a man of his type in my life. He was bare-chested and wore a pair of shorts. He was also bare-footed. His left arm was in a big bandage. He behaved as though he did not take notice of my presence. Then with the key in his hand he walked away. After pondering over the whole incidence for some time, I decided to continue my journey in the same direction he took.

After walking for about half an hour, someone called me from behind and said, "Take this key and go back to open the door for them. They are suffocating to death". I turned and politely told the man that he had better give the key to the police as this was the duty of the police. Then he said, "The police have not got the spiritual power that you have. If you don't lead this crusade, no one can".

Then I received the key from him and returned. On my way back, I had the intuition that I would meet the man on the way. Minutes later, I saw him with bow and arrow ready to shoot at me. I also saw smaller men, who bore resemblance to the giant, and were also holding bows and arrows right in my path. But I was not scared because as soon as I received the key in the dream a power entered me and I felt stronger than he, so, while I was still going toward him, a power lifted me very high up from the ground and propelled me fast across the spot where they were and slowly lowered me on to the ground and urged me to continue my way. This happened twice.

When I remembered that they were suffocating to death, I began to double up then I heard a mighty crowd singing in the sky. The lyrics of the song was, "A cross will be on your shoulder as you head towards the mountain of liberation". In fact, this was the most melodious song that I have ever heard. I hurried up and said to myself that they were suffocating to death. While still running, I woke up. The whole dream seemed real to me. So I wanted to put my hand into my pocket to bring out the key when I realized that it was a dream. But the anxiety to open the door for them has remained in me since.

I was then teaching in a Government Secondary School in Lome, called, Lycee du 2 Fevrier. When I went to school the following day I could not teach because the whole dream was featuring prominently in my thoughts.

I am, therefore, still burdened to liberate all fetish slaves from the various shrines of Trokosi, Yewhe, Agbosu and Korku cults. At the appropriate time, I will expose all these terrible cults to the whole world.

FESLIM is capable of liberating all these fetish slaves regardless of the shrines' powers. Hence, FESLIM is passionately appealing to all Churches, women's organizations, Embassies, other NGOs and individuals to give us financial and logistic support to enable us achieve this noble goal. I now yield the rest of my time to Rev. Kwasi Torde Torvike of Kwasi Torvike Evangelistic Association for a brief video presentation about the Trokosi system.

Thank you.

Trokosi: The Experience of a Family

Rev. Edwin Kwabla Agbanu

Chairperson, Seminar participants Ladies and Gentlemen, I am going to speak to you on the topic "What is Trokosi System" in my capacity as a person who is witnessing the obnoxious Trokosi System destroy my dear sister, the third after me.

Definition

What is Trokosi System? Trokosi System is the holding of an innocent girl or a woman in captivity for the sins committed by her family member of whom the victim may not even have any knowledge.

In the early part of 1954 my family at Mafi Mediage in the North Tongu district, experienced four deaths within a month, that is, we lost my aunt, a sister, a brother and my dear mother in that order.

My families, like any other Ghanaian family, do not accept that death is part of the biological process, that is, if you are born you are bound to die. As a result they had to consult a diviner to determine the causes of these deaths. They were told by the diviner that the deaths came as a result of the failure of one of our fore-fathers to fulfill a promise he made to the deity at Volo in the North Tongu district. This fore-father of ours when he was going to one of the wars against the Ashantis called on this deity to protect him. He promised that after he had returned from the war safely he would thank this deity. But he failed to do so. What was to be done to stop these deaths was to send someone to the shrine at Volo for life to pacify the deity there.

Fellow seminar participants, when those who went to consult the diviner returned, they told the family the outcome of their consultation. Since they were all adherents of Traditional Religion and superstitious in outlook, they accepted what the diviner had said as the truth. The family decided on a day to meet to decide upon the one to send to the shrine at Volo to atone for the sin of that fore-father of ours. When they met, a lot was cast and it fell on my sister.

My sister, Akle, was between the ages of 7 and 8 years when in her innocence she was taken to the shrine against her will to start her slavery. Fellow seminar participants, I say that my poor innocent sister became a slave and she is still a slave in the sense that, the moment she arrived at the shrine at that tender age, she lost all her God given rights as a human being. Her arrival at the shrine signaled the fact that she has become the wife of the leader of the shrine called "Togbe". She married someone she did not like or love. She was going to be forced to have sex. She had no right to attend school. So you see, my sister has not attended school. Schooling which is a source of liberation, transformation and an eye-opener has been denied my sister.

Another ugly part of Trokosi system is that so long as my sister remains at the shrine, it is the responsibility of my family to care for her. It is the duty of my family to clothe, feed and take her to hospital when she is sick. The number of children she has with Togbe should be cared for by my family. Fellow seminar participants, Togbe, the shrine leader, has a singular right, that is, he is to impregnate my sister and after he has done that job he has nothing to do with the woman by way of feeding or giving her medical care.

However, the children so produced by my sister have to bear his name. Furthermore, fellow seminar participants, the tradition regarding trokosi system in Mafi traditional area is that no Mafi citizen is allowed to marry a trokosi girl. So you see that my sister has become an object that should be feared in Mafi traditional area. Because of the stigma attached to trokosi system in Mafi, my sister is not allowed to stay in my father's house for a long time. This is because that is not the right place for her to stay. Her rightful place to stay is the shrine. As a result of this she always lives outside Mafi state. My dear fellow seminar participants, you see how trokosi system has destroyed my sister's warm relationship with her dear family members.

When I returned from a journey I had made some few months ago, my sister came to me. She told me she could no longer bear the heavy burdens trokosi system has put on her. That she was going to end it all by taking poison. All the people of her age group, girls as well as boys, some of them are honorable teachers and nurses and others lawyers living responsible lives as men and women of integrity but she is languishing under the yoke of trokosi system. My dear sister Akle is now an alcoholic.

Three weeks ago when I went home I met my sister heavily drunk. I told her to stop alchoholism. Listen to the answer she gave me:

She said:- "I cannot stop alcoholism: so far as I am a trokosi. I am no more a human being. I have no place to lay my head. What a disgrace my family has put on me." My dear fellow seminar participants, trokosi system is akin to the Obnoxious Apartheid system, which existed in South Africa some years ago. Trokosi system is an institution, which works against the development of women and should be stopped. It is also a symbol of backwardness, because it is insensitive to human feeling and should be abolished.

Madam chairperson, fellow seminar participants, ladies and gentlemen;

We are about to enter the next Millennium. This shows how advanced in age the world is to be able to discern what militates against her peace and progress. Trokosi System is an enemy of women.

I am done. Thank you.

Editors' Note

After this speech, his sister told her own story in Ewe and as most of the participants spoke the language, there was much weeping and much empathetic non-verbal expressions. The gathering was moved spontaneously to begin donating money for her to try trading to rehabilitate herself. They also resolved to conduct further probes into this plight of their community. Hence the follow up of Peki and Adidome.

A Christian perspective on trokosi

G.K. Akorli

Introduction

Trokosi system refers to a practice in which virgins called 'kosi' or servants served a number of years in the shrine of a deity called 'Tro' as a reparation of offences committed by their parents, relatives or a family member. The offences committed may be stealing, murder, adultery or fornication against 'Tro'. Land and chieftaincy cases may also call for this sacrifice. At times the girls serve in the shrine not because of offences committed by their family member but as a thanks-offering for a fortune which was believed to come from 'Tro'.

This 'Tro' is called 'Troxovi' which means a "deity that takes a child". There are many shrines of this 'Troxovi' at the Southern sector of Volta Region. Precisely they are found in villages such as Fodzoku, Torgome, Dorfor, Volo, Mepe, Battor, Mafi-Dugame, Avakpedome, Bakpa, Vume, Tefle, Sokpoe, Fieve, Agave, Agbozume and Klikor.

Background History

Tradition has it that this deity 'Troxovi' was brought from Notsie in Togo during the time when Anlos and Tongus at Southern sector of Volta Region migrated to their present place of settlement. 'Troxovi was a 'war-god' which the people believed was the deity that protected them during wars and led them during the time of migration.

The people did not only rely on this 'Troxovi' for protection but also regarded it as the source of their unity as a community. They therefore offered sacrifices at shrines to avert calamities and as thanks-offerings for their protection from enemies, other divinities and evil spirits.

During the ancient time, we were told, goats and not virgins were offered at the shrines as reparation for offences committed and also for protection and prosperity. But as time went on this practice of offering goats changed probably because of economic gains of the shrine owners and the priests. The maidens or '*kosi*' in the shrines of Mafi-Dugame and Avakpedome are sometimes referred to as 'goats'. This actually confirmed the fact that goats were sacrificed during the ancient times.

What Happens in the Shrines

The maidens or '*kosi*' serving in the shrines are regarded as the wives of the 'Troxovi' and therefore have no right whatever to have sexual relationship with any other man apart from the priest of the shrine. The priest is at liberty to have sexual relationship with any *kosi* even against her wish. When the girls are put in the family way their maintenance during and after the pregnancy becomes their responsibility of the victims' parents or families. As a result, the priests of the various shrines have given birth to many children from these unfortunate and vulnerable *kosi*.

The *kosi* serving in the shrines are used as cheap labour. They work on the farms of the priest and shrine owners, but even they have no right to enjoy the fruits of their labour. Their parents or families are always responsible for their feeding and clothing in addition to the issues (children) they have with the Priest. They head-carry the produce of the farm on foot to the market for sale.

The victims *(kosi)* have no freedom of religion or worship and association. They are forced to worship the 'Troxovi' even if they have completed their period of service. The practice is that even those who complete their period of service report annually at the shrine for some rituals at the expense of their parents or families. Once you are '*kosi*' you remain kosi forever even if you complete your terms of service.

The maidens or *'kosi'* and their children have no access to formal education. The *'kosi'* have no chance of going to school because of the services they render to the priest and shrine owners. The children suffer the same because the priest who is supposed to be their father refuses to look after them.

Christianity and the Trokosi System

The situation of 'Trokosi' in the shrine is more than that of a slave. In the Biblical times certain special regulations applied to female Hebrew slaves. For instance, when a Hebrew slave was designated as a wife for the master's son, she was to be treated with the due rights of daughters. Even if the son took another wife, there was to be no diminishing of her sustenance. Exd. 21 : 7 - 11. The law also protected slaves from brutalities. Exd. 21: 20, 32.

The first century Christians did not take a stand against the then government in matters of slavery. This was because the institution of slavery had the protection of the imperial government. The slave masters respected the legal rights of the slaves. That was why St. Paul sent back the runaway slave, Onesimus, to the master. (Philem. 10 - 17.)

In the 'Trokosi' system, the '*trokosi*' in the shrines are not given protection and privileges. They are given any treatment at the discretion of the priest and the shrine owners. As already discussed feeding and clothing become the responsibilities of their parents or families even though the **trokosi** serve their masters in many ways.

Christianity therefore cannot compromise with the Trokosi system since what goes on in the shrines is incompatible with the Christian virtues and the teachings of the Bible. In Christianity all persons regardless of their social status enjoy the same standing. According to St. Paul, all people are anointed by the same spirit and thus share in the same hope as members of one body. (1 Cor. 12: 12 - 13). Some schools of thought argued that they did not see anything wrong with the Trokosi system because to them, the girls or virgins given out into slavery in the shrine were regarded as 'sacrificial lambs' whose services would avert the calamities which would befall the family for the offences committed by a member.

To this school of thought similar sacrifices were made during the Old Testament era when the life of an animal or human being was sacrificed as ransom in place of the life of a sinner. (Lev. 17: 11, Gen. 22, Heb. 9: 13). The fact that Abraham was asked to sacrifice his only son Isaac to God confirmed the fact that human sacrifice was going on. But we saw from the story that God Himself provided ram instead of Isaac for the sacrifice. This showed that God was actually against the sacrifice of human being in any form for atonement. Jesus Christ, our Lord, paid the final price by shedding His precious blood for the remission of the sin of humankind. By this single act of Christ we are saved and our sins are forgiven.

Trokosi system therefore is just a traditional institution to punish innocent virgins or girls for the wrongs done by other people. The Bible said "the soul that sins shall die" (Ezk. 18: 4) and so it is morally improper for anybody or group of people to use these girls or Trokosi as a reparation. In addition to the reparation for the offences committed it is of much economic gain to the priests and the shrine owners.

True sacrifice of oneself for the life of others must come from 'free will' and not by force as in the Trokosi system.

LIBERATIVE MOVES

Contributions of Church and Society Towards the Liberation of the Trokosi Victim

J.A.K. Amenorhu

The term Trokosi victim is perhaps sacrosanct and appears to defy precise definition because it has for a long time been shrouded in mystery and abject secrecy. For over a century, no one dared to question its existence; in fact any avowed critic was rendered impotent to raise a finger of protest openly or in the quiet because the system remained fearsome and terrifying; indeed, a no-go area. Thank Heavens, the day has dawned, the season has arrived and the time has come for human knowledge 'to be updated with the solo work of the angel at midnight on Christmas, chorused by the Heavenly Choir with the Divine Message: " Glory be to God in highest, Peace on Earth, Goodwill to mankind".

Ladies and Gentlemen, that is why it has been possible for you to belong to a most seasoned Institution clothed with the authority to question the existence of Trokosi, much more launch a furious campaign towards the liberation and rehabilitation of the system's victims. This is precisely why we have all assembled here as people of various religious and social backgrounds to work towards a common goal.

I am sure that those of you who come from areas where this heinous crime is not practised have to depend upon briefs to update your knowledge on the system. Fortunately, you are in North Tongu, the citadel or nerve center of the system in Tongu where the practice boasts of the existence of the greatest number of shrines in the Southern Sector of the Volta Region. So you see, Madam Organizer, you could not have chosen a better venue for an all embracing forum. I dare say that most of the people, who are going to feature in the programme, are giants in their own rights and are prepared to give you the benefit of their vision.

As I speak, I still can visualize the spectacle of my maternal aunt who was forcefully initiated into the diabolical system and graduated with dishonor recounting her remorseful experiences amidst torrents of tears rolling down her four-score and eight years' old cheeks. What a human tragedy! The last straw that broke the camel's back has been that the male children born of Trokosi have been disenfranchised or stripped of the right to ascend to our clan stool. When that poor woman had cried, God had wept.

The Genesis/Historical Perspective of the System

Mr. Chairperson, Eminent resource persons, Fellow participants, Ladies and Gentlemen I have tried to organize an incursion into the hitherto no-go area on the authority of Prof. Fiawoo, once Head of Sociology Department, University of Ghana. In his periscope of the study of West African Societies he briefly explains the origin of the practice. He explains that during the mass exodus of Ewes from their original ancestral roots in Notsie (Ewe Diaspora) in about the late 17th century into the 18th century ostensibly to free themselves from the diabolical and tyrannical rule of King Agorkorli, the various autonomous clan States moved to new settlements in various directions in unique defense arrangements.

These were as follows:

Military Leadership

The various contingents were led by the Field Marshals (Avadada wo) and Field Captains – (Ademega wo.) The membership of this group was largely drawn from time-tested hunters as well as people who excelled in the art of bravery in battle. They provided military intelligence and engaged the enemies while awaiting re -enforcement from the other fronts behind them.

Priests

These are the powerful Priests (Tronuorwo) who were also drawn from people who exhibited skill, art and science of herbal and general traditional/spiritual medicine and charms. Prominent in their category are the sorcerers, soothsayers and those who practise the art of divination in pitched up tents constructed with palm fronds and branches. Because of limitations imposed on them by tradition, their movements are restricted to their roles and entirely divorced from secular matters. Included in the group are a large retinue of old women, men, p*riests,* priestesses, slaves - Trokosi and "vestal virgins" (Troxoviviwo).

Traditional Rulers

The third migrant group was led by the Traditional Rulers-kings and the *mankralos (Afetofiawo)*. It consisted of Royal Clansmen of the various chiefs and array of elders, men and women who serve the chiefs and above all, the militias or various *Asafo* groups who guard the moving community from the rear in the event of attack by enemies. Infact historians, sociologists and anthropologists assert that the migratory history of the Ewe in Ghana, Togo, Benin, Nigeria date as far back as the late 17th century and followed similar defense arrangements.

Vestiges of the Trokosi System

The Shrines as they exist today are the replica of the established institutions of the various deities through which media the Supreme Deity Mawuga, Sogbolisa, Okitikata, the source of Life, is reached. Just after the 2nd World War, a conglomeration of these syncretic cults emerged and became lucrative practice for people of all walks of life, prominent among the known ones in North and South Tongu are as follows:

Location		Name of Cult
Agave	-	Adzem
Mafi	-	Avakpe, Kole, Geta etc.
Dorfor	-	Koklofu, Badzi, Tsaduma etc
Tefle	-	Koti, Adzem etc.
Volo	-	Me, 'Lomo etc.
Bakpa	-	Tsaduma, Evens etc.
Battor	-	Atigo etc.
Mepe	-	Adido etc.
Anlo	-	Ahogbato etc.
Ada	-	Kole etc.

Distinguished personalities, fellow participants, ladies and gentlemen, the list provided above is not exhaustive. Having been a student re-searcher, on syncretic cults i.e. Yeve, Tigare and Afakaka (Oracular consultation), I have embraced the historical assertion that, the system has survived two and a half Centuries into the 21st Century. I am of the conviction that the problem of Trokosi could best be tackled on the State/Church Co-operation basis using the series of University Research findings as medium to launch final assault on the existence of the dragon.

The System in Practice

Maternal Aunt's Experience as Case Study

One day, my aunt's mother was involved in a petty row with one of her 4 co-wives over an allegation of gossiping about her barreness which it was alleged was the result of her witchcraft. My aunt's mother protested vehemently against the allegation claiming innocence. The rival who had an opportunity to wreak her vengeance upon her quickly swore the great fetish oath of the area, claiming damages of one guinea (one pound, one shilling) one live ram, one goat, two white cockerels, twelve bottles of spirits and a host of purification rites items.

Although several witnesses bore false witness against the defendant during the trial, the arbitration ended in further confusion with the result that a trial by ordeal was ordered by the panel. The plaintiff refused to go through the rituals first just as the defendant did also. The co-wife was reported to have bribed the arbitrators who pronounced judgment in favor of the plaintiff. She was to pay a total fine of One Pound, Eleven Shillings and Six Pence in addition to the items mentioned above.

It was like the day "a voice was heard in Rama, weeping and great mourning Rachael weeping for her children because they are not". The grief stricken woman wept her heart out refusing to be consoled but alas! The die was cast and my aunt, a rather meek and innocent young lady was led like a sheep without a shepherd into the fetish shrine to serve as the reparation fee due to the fetish priest to atone for a crime she was innocent of.

A close examination of the victim, as she passes through the gates into the shrine, and as she leaves the society which is to protect her virginity and advance her human rights behind her, lends credence to the fact that she enters a world of misery, suffering and dehumanization. A few examples may suffice here:-

She is deprived of the right to be fed, educated, clothed and properly housed.

Her freedom of movement, speech, and to join social groups of her choice curtailed.

She is forced into an early unprepared, unnegotiated marriage, marital union not by choice nor consent is a flagrant violation of the woman's birth and civil rights.

By the victim's work ethics, she is not only exploited but equally undergoes mental agony and torture. The sudden change in her mode of dressing, appearance and observance of personal hygiene in the midst of the large array of the inmates creates not only an emotional distress but equally a loss of ego and personal decency.

Ladies and Gentlemen, if Ghanaian womanhood is to be protected and preserved this outmoded and outrageous practice must be prohibited throughout Ghana, West Africa and Africa as a whole.

My brothers and sisters, this is a naked instance of what the situation was like at the time and you would wonder if social justice ever existed in the lives of human beings who were the champions of this monstrous practice. The rest of the gruesome story of service in servitude at the shrine is told in glittering alphabets by Rev. Mark Wisdom who examined the system more closely and provided an etymological analysis of the term *trokosi* as it existed in those bleak days. Suppose you are in authority to command even the sun to stand still, what would have been your reaction to this system?

Socio-Cultural and Psychological Perspective on the System

Sociologists believe that the sum total of man's learned ways of behavior shape his personality in society. Again by nature, the human being is a gregarious animal and that his judgment on issues is based on stimulus response process in his community and his perception of others. In other words, public opinion of the Trokosi system is based on the perception of the victims on one hand and their public relations/communication with the outside world on the other.

The ultimate question one should ponder over is; why has it taken the Ghanaian society i.e. individually and as a group such a long time to call for the abolition of the system?

Society is an agent of socialization, it needs to be, since it is made up of many individuals set in family units. Society has acquired the function of influencing both the individuals and the groups. One clear observation of how this is achieved is the group's dynamics that promote cohesiveness or 'we-ness' in social and religious settings. Group's dynamics i.e. is the most powerful factors capable of gingering up mob action towards the achievement of an objective.

Secondly, society also has the basic role of coercing individuals, families and other groups to conform to the society's approved norms. Folkways, practices, conventions and statutes are in place to draw attention to as well as remove unpopular regimes. Persons in authority and decision-making are respected and upheld as they effect a mandate or institute changes that promote social progress, development, peace and stability in society.

Distinguished Participants, Ladies and Gentlemen, I mentioned earlier on in this treatise that the Trokosi system was an impregnable and veritable religious institution, a fearsome and a " no-go -area" for both governments and non-governmental authorities because of freedom of religion. But why has it become necessary for the abolition of the system even to the extent of liberating the victims from the shrines where the custom is practised?

First, society has become aware of the abominable and inhuman practices, involved in trokosi. Secondly, modern society has the basic and fundamental right to reject through mass demonstration, customary or religious practices that do not augur well for people. That is why the world will forever and ever remain grateful to the leadership of the bodies/institutions that are struggling to eliminate the practice. Here are a few of them:

- Fetish Slaves Liberation Movement
- Missions International
- International Needs
- Commission on Human Rights and Administrative Justice (CHRAJ)
- Institute of Women in Religion and Culture.

and all others that featured in the CRUSADE for the Liberation and Rehabilitation of the Trokosi victims in Tongu, Anlo and Ada. Glory to God in the highest, Peace on Earth and Goodwill to mankind; I say *Ayekoo! Miawoe le agbedo wom.*

Contributions of Church and Society

In conclusion, I wish to draw attention to the fact that the crusade to liberate and rehabilitate the Trokosi Victims is not yet over until it is over. I have argued that a society has a fundamental role of influencing or pressurizing the individual, families, clans, social and religious groups to conform to its approved norms, folkways, practices or statute in order to maintain peace, justice, security and stability in its domain. In this vein I commend highly the efforts of the various Non-Governmental Organizations (NGOS) and other organizations through whose efforts the liberation and rehabilitation of Trokosi Victims have become a reality. Currently, the efforts of the Institute of Women in Religion and Culture in organizing this four-day Seminar to step up the enthusiasm of society towards the crusade is in the right direction.

It is satisfying to note that for once our distinguished female counterparts have come down from what used to be "ivory tower" to identify themselves with the plight of the downtrodden in Ghanaian society.

Finally, I wish to express my heartfelt gratitude to the membership of the Institute for its bold and progressive effort in reminding society of its avowed aim to protect and safeguard the freedom and civil liberties of the victims of this intolerable customary practice in Ghana and also for the invitation to me to feature in this programme. I wish to commend also their efforts for the attention and assistance of the District Assemblies in coming over unto Macedonia to help, for in this moral co-operation and assistance lies the future of the builders of the nation of tomorrow.

Long live the Institute of Women In Religion and Culture, Trinity Theological Seminary Legon,

Long live the Liberation Movement,

Long live Ghana.

Thank you

PART 11

FIRST PAN-AFRICAN CONFERENCE

Papers from the Conference

A call for Jubilee for African Women - A Concept Paper on the research/study on the effects of Globalization on African Women.

by Omega Bula

Introduction

The emphasis of this proposal is to call on the Circle of Concerned African Women Theologians and the Institute of African Women in Religion and Culture, through their focus on Religion and Culture to **engage** in a study/ research on the impact of the global economic crisis on African women and to convey the urgency and the centrality of engaging with economics (the present global-market dominated ideology and its evils) as a matter of faith.

This initial concept paper will serve only as a proposed framework for discussion and a possible point of departure in the work we do on the impact of globalization. The quality of the project will be determined by the energy and enthusiasm, insights and contributions African women theologians will bring into the project.

What is globalization? And why are theologians and religious bodies called to respond to globalization and neo-liberalism?

There is no clear agreement as to what globalization means. "i.e. depends on what we are talking about," a friend of mine who has spent a lot of time writing on the subject said at the beginning of his presentation. He went on to explain that globalization is a process that cannot be ignored in terms of reflection and analysis because it marks a decisive change in the forces that drive the world economy[1]. Globalization refers to the process of the integration of the world markets. There is pressure to compete in a free market economy - to produce and sell for profit, with rules and regulations that apply every where, no matter the level of development of the particular economy. This process is giving shape to the integration of financial markets, global governance, access and use of technology especially information technology, and the development of a few people that hold and manage power at the world level. The common rhetoric is that this process will bring economic growth for all. What is more evident however is the growing imbalances among the rich and the poor.

For Africa, with two thirds of the countries that carry the debt burden, the implementation of structural adjustments (SAPS) as an instrument for globalization (i.e. enable the ailing African economies recover so that they can participate in the market economy) has resulted in an increasing number of the poor, with growing unemployment and underemployment, the reduction or stagnation of earnings, and in many cases of diminishing access to education, health, housing, food and security. A growing number are excluded from meaningful participation in determining their livelihood, and in benefiting from the social benefits generated from the wealth of their countries. So while disregarding the traditional boundaries, and the autonomy of nations and cultures, globalization marginalizes, excludes, socially disintegrates communities and has contributed to the increase of violence and civil conflicts. Fridah Muyale-Manenji has summed up the impact of globalization in Africa as 'a further undermining of the internal, national productive capacity, social security and democratic integrity of these (African) countries.'

The impact of the current economic policies on women's rights and women's dignity has been critical, and therefore the focus of this project in calling for a Jubilee for Women. The poor of the world, and especially the majority of women, have been turned into slaves of the free market which has been elevated to a status of human control - that there are no alternatives to the current trend. The market has been imbued with a divine status, with its own laws and disciplines, high priests, and apologists for a distorted theology of sacrifice and theology of prosperity. According to Paul Gifford, it is a theology of conquest, the promised land, individualism, chosen people, abundance and laissez faire..... it is a theology that is destroying African traditions, value system and cultures, plundering the resources of the continent and set, not only Africa but the whole world, in collision course with nature.'

The concept of jubilee

Jubilee is an all encompassing vision of social and ecological justice. In the Biblical tradition it was the time which occurred every 50 years - at which time slaves were to be released, debts were to be forgiven, wealth (land) was to be equitably shared or redistributed among all, and the land was to be given rest from its labor. (Leviticus 25 and 27). As the world approaches the year 2,000 a hopeful vision for the Jubilee has been called - globally and ecumenically. It is a call proclaimed in solidarity and partnership with those who struggle most in the global economy, with a focus on the cancellation of debts for the most highly indebted countries in the world.

What is the hope for African women in this Jubilee initiative? How will the Jubilee for women become a reality? How can we continue to build on the gains of the Ecumenical Decade - Churches in Solidarity with Women?

Goals of the project

Through the researched study of particular key issues of concern, the Project will seek to make a contribution to the understanding of the profound dimensions in which we are all being co-opted into the idolization of the market economy as the solution to all problems. How can we as African women begin to confront this perspective with a sense of urgency given the experience of the market economy? For the majority of African people and especially of African women the effect of free economy has been that of increasing poverty, cultural and religious oppression, suffering and exclusion, violence and disruption of family life. How can African Women Theologians contribute to the processes of awakening and resistance that Christ calls us to undertake?

Some specific goals for us could be:-

- To enhance the understanding of the impact of economic injustice on African women
- To empower women in their search for survival strategies
- To enable theological reflection that will help communities make the connection between faith and economics
- To influence economic policy from a gender perspective
- To provide concrete tools and resources which can be used in deepening the understanding of economics as a matter of faith
- To call individuals and communities to engage in concrete actions/ interventions e.g. the Jubilee 2000 Campaign
- To hear/learn from concerned African women theologians, their perspective/theological insights on faith and economics

- To contribute to the transformation processes - from brokenness to wholeness both individually and in community with others as women witness to Christ's ministry of love, justice and reconciliation.

Core concerns

Concerned with the debt crisis in Africa: Some ideas-

From a theological perspective, build on the existing research base on gender and economic reforms, on instruments being used to address the debt crisis in Africa e.g. structural adjustment programs, international agreements on trade, etc., with the purpose of expanding and disseminating knowledge on the relationship between economic reform processes and gender inequality.

Concerned with the feminization of poverty some ideas-

Studying poverty resistance strategies which women are employing in everyday life - what are these, how are women articulating these in relation to their faith? What learnings are there?

How is culture changing due to globalization and why? e.g. in male-female relationships/roles and destinies, access to and use of wealth, division of labor, experiences of violence against women, access to education and health etc. What are the constraints on women's lives and women's empowerment?

How has the feminization of poverty impacted on men's control of women's bodies? Attitudes to sexuality?

Concerned for the well-being of children and young adults. Some ideas:-

To make connections between the feminization of poverty and the povertisation of motherhood.

Children are often the silent victims of the economic crisis, violence, cultural disruptions, environmental degradation, etc. A focus on the production of research that explores these connections would strengthen the advocacy for children's rights.

Developing entry level resources that will help young adults/youth articulate their own concerns about poverty and other issues, the idea of writing tracts and cartoon type material that touch on the real life issues being faced by youth has already been muted in the Circle.

Highlighting issues which impact on the well-being of the girl child concerned to unmask oppressive theology that invokes the 'idolatry' and 'worship' of the free market; the sacrifice of human life in the name of economic growth.

Some ideas: Religion has been known to influence people. Collect and critically analyze the prosperity sermons with groups of women and young adults. Offer open fora on the meaning of sacrifice in religion and its implications for economic life.

Concerned for the well-being of the earth, some ideas:

Ecological degradation has come in the wake of profit and as people in poor countries struggle to coexist with nature - what is the relationship between ecological degradation and poverty? e.g. diminishing access to land, cash cropping Vs food production impact on traditional methods of agriculture and loss of indigenous knowledge, and seeds etc.

Structure and format of papers

It is critical that this process gives voice and enables African women to address the issues in a personal and experiential way. A model commonly used in the ecumenical community and which links us to our Biblical tradition is that of the epistle or letter format.

This format will enable the writers to resist the academic treatment of the content, and help the reader in the process of demystifying economics, so that many of us can claim economics as what we do in our everyday lives and therefore can impact what happens in the management of God's household and how.

The powerfulness of this format in communicating the issues of economic injustice lies in the possibility to incorporate the strengths of our cultural experiences of survival, our history, our stories, our dreams, our songs and prayers, our analysis and our theological reflection.

Writers will be encouraged to use the 'see, judge, act' format

Theological underpinnings

A compelling invitation to work in partnership with a God of life accompanied by the unmasking of the deadening ideology. An emphasis that victory is on the side of justice, even though the struggle is not over, that the jubilee tradition offers us the chance for a new beginning, a sense of hope.

Given our focus on women's experience of the economy, it will be important to evoke female imagery of God, in symbols and language.

There are a multitude of challenges and opportunities but we need to be *alert, read the signs of the times, watch and pray.*

TO GUIDE OUR DISCUSSION OF THIS CONCEPT PAPER

- What do you affirm in this proposal?
- What improvements need to be made?
- What questions or concerns do you have?
- What implications do you see for the Circle and the Institute?
- What are the next steps?

Nigerian Economic Depression: It's impact on the Christian Women

R-M. Owanikin

Introduction

Nigeria became an independent country from the British Colonial Government in 1960. The economy inherited was relatively stable and vibrant but politically there were cries amongst the three dominant political parties namely; the Action Group (AG), National Council for Nigerian Citizen (NCNC) and the Northern People's Congress. (NPC).

The political climate was bedevilled with thuggery, arson, killing, embezzlement, corruption, fraud and other vices. The economy of the country was adversely affected and this consequently led to the military coup d'etat and seizure of power in January 1963. After more than three decades of military rule until the May 29, 1999 restoration of democratic governance, the economic state of the nation is yet to stabilize positively. The indices show that Nigerian's per capita income is low. The currency (Naira) is getting increasingly devalued and the quality of life worsens with a prevailing and alarming inflationary rate. In other words, economic depression is a major symptom of political instability.

Virtually, all facets of the Nigerian society has suffered from the resultant cankerworm of corruption and poverty. The Western world suspect the integrity of Nigerians. In foreign countries, Nigerians are kept under tight surveillance. Interestingly, the economic depression may have contributed to the upsurge of Christian activity in the country. Not only is there a globalization of Pentecostal revival, proliferation of churches has also become dominant. The crucial question thus arises: what is the role of religion particularly Christianity in addressing the problem of economic depression, corruption and survival of people in Nigeria? This is the problem which this paper attempts to examine. In doing so, the study will focus on the feminist perspective. Women occupy a privileged position of watching over this country. We will discuss the causes of economic depression as well as attempt to proffer solutions to them. We will also consider the practicable virtues in Christian women which can contribute to the search for solutions to Nigeria's socio-political and economic problems.

Problems and Effects of a Depressed Economy

The Problem

Morality is the value of human behavior, right or wrong conduct, it is closely related to the Greek ethos (ethics). Moral behavior is thus dictated and governed by good conduct, discipline, accountability, responsibility and general virtuous behavior. The successive governments of Nigeria since its independence have not exhibited these virtues in the act of governance hence the apparent deterioration of the nation's life in virtually every ramification[5]. This ugly situation has many problems for the state and the individual. The rate at which crime is being perpetrated is alarming. The sad thing is that the leadership is not excluded. Government functionaries aid, abet and perpetuate crime. The print and the electronics media alarm us daily on the rate at which lives and properties are wasted by robbers. People's houses have become more like prison yards. This is because iron bars and burglar proof are erected in such a way that so many inner doors would have to be opened before inhabitants could get out.

The bad state of the economy has impacted negatively on marriages. Infidelity in marriages has become common, eventually leading to broken homes. The rate of divorce is also increasing. Extra marital relations are often motivated by economic and financial needs.

Physically, some economically deprived husbands with unsettled mind can hardly perform effectively in sexual acts. When it persists, it could ensnare the deprived partner to yearn for this biological need in an illegitimate manner. When this is discovered, the implications could result in divorce.

Financially, a situation where a husband cannot fulfill the basic needs of feeding the family also encourages infidelity. Some wives have entangled themselves by seeking solutions illegitimately.

Injustice is another serious problem. The confidence of the ordinary citizen in the Judiciary is waning gradually. Not only is justice expensive to obtain, the rich appear to be above the law while the poor masses remain down-trodden. Many people who are unemployed are desperate to survive and have gone into all sorts of shady deals, armed robbery, hired assassins, political thugs, drug addicts and drug peddlers, while some members of the armed forces are on their pay roll for protection.

The problem of corruption is more endemic. This evil has eaten deep into the fabric of the society, it will take the mercy of God to rescue us as a nation. This is because corruption runs through every strata of society from top to bottom including the military leaders, politicians, businessmen, teachers, clergymen and students. The rate at which bribery takes place in this land is worrisome. Policemen no longer have shame. They openly demand and receive bribe. Officers of the Federal Road Safety are now becoming vulnerable. Other problems can be summarized as bad values, juvenile delinquency, drug addiction, prostitution, greed, lack of peace being the most obvious ones.

The effects

The depressed state of the economy in Nigeria has badly affected virtually all her sectors. The political life of the country is in a mess. The military on the pretext of salvaging the situation has enriched itself at the expense of enduring democracy in Nigeria. The coups and counter-coups are evidence of the insatiable urge in each of the actors for self-enrichment. The political life of the nation continues to be the scape goat. People's confidence in high expectation of dividends from democratic government in Nigeria is gradually waning. The unstable political situation of the country has subjected her to ridicule in the arena of foreign powers. For example on November 12 1995, John Major, the then Prime Minister of the United Kingdom on Cable News Network, announced that Nigeria was suspended for two years from the Commonwealth of Nations and that if she did not transit into democratic rule, she will be expelled outright. This was a major dent on the country's pride and sovereignty. The so called 'giant of Africa" was being pummelled left, right and center with sanctions that will have serious consequences for her survival as a nation and that of her citizens, while it persisted.

Socially, life in Nigeria is still quite unstable. The educational sector of the country is fast losing its integrity, value and respect. With the strikes, unpaid staff salaries, students being killed by uniformed men, secret cults on some of the Secondary Schools and University Campuses, immorality among students, the problem seem intractable. At the domestic level commodities are so expensive, transportation fares are up as a result of the mis-managed petroleum resources and attendant scarcity of the commodities, house rentage is rising by the year, many Nigerians in their thousands have been retrenched from their jobs, and when they make attempts to look for another, they meet a brick wall. It is becoming outrageously expensive to live in Nigeria. Most salary earners earn their salary to pay debts because the situation is such that what they receive is not enough to cope with their daily and natural needs.

The value of the Nigerian currency is nothing. As at 10 March 2001, the Naira exchanged at N118 to an American Dollar in the autonomous financial market. Because of this devalued state, life has become unbearable for most Nigerians and so most Nigerian youths are desperate to leave the country for 'better' living as many have already done. Some professionals in all and especially in areas where the needs are yet to be met in the country, like medicine and other sciences, have left the country to seek greener pastures in foreign countries. The greed to make money by all means has led to adulteration of medicinal drugs. Some people have been caught selling fake and at times expired drugs and other substances different from the label the container carries.

The religious angle is not spared. The need and the quest for peace and solution by some people in Nigeria have exposed them to false prophets who themselves are all looking for a way to cushion their financial tension and had therefore resorted to deceit as a way of life. This situation has ridiculed the integrity and the genuine nature of religion. This is because it then becomes difficult for some people to distinguish between true and false prophets. Out of depression, some have been cheated, demoralized and deceived by these false prophets. All these and more are the painful effects of the declining state of our economy.

The Role of the Christian Woman in Revamping a Depressed Economy

Economic depression is a problem that must be collectively addressed by the entire citizenry. What are the specific roles which the Christian woman can play in the quest for moral, economic and spiritual sanity in Nigeria?

Our proposition is based on the fact that the Christian woman has unique potentials which qualify her to be at the fore-front.

For the role of the Christian woman to be effective, she needs to impart good manners to her children right from the cradle of child nurturing. Unfortunately, some women have failed in this aspect as they often neglect their children. This gives rise to broken homes and child abuse. The Christian woman should not allow the distracting demands of the present society to adversely affect her proper role as a Christian. The role of the family is the most crucial of all microcosms that constitute the Nigerian agents of change.

In some churches today, the position of women has greatly improved. This increasing privileged status should enable the Christian woman to carry out her moral and spiritual teachings effectively. Many women are now functioning as teachers, preachers, church founders etc. The Christian woman can effectively usher moral and spiritual re-orientation into Nigeria by not allowing the popular adage of "if you cannot beat them, you join them" to govern her life and that of her family.

Her mission should be distinct from the exploitative syndrome which has become a predominant aspect of our society today. The open display of wealth in the presence of people in the society who are suffering economic hardship is worrisome. The Christian who is blessed with riches should make it a point of duty to assist the poor. This will reduce the problems that often come from the hungry members of the society. Furthermore, the Christian woman should teach the importance of obeying the laws of the land. This is because without obedience to legitimate authority, life would become meaningless in an anarchical society. The best way by which we can successfully carry out this function is by showing good example, for without good example, any teaching and preaching would only result in futility. Women must distance themselves from vices which tarnish the integrity of the nation.

Women should also undergo training to be able to handle sensitive situations that require ethical standards. Due to the fact that church and society have learnt to forget the presence of women, the Christian women should fight for government welfare support for the homes, privileges for education of women and provision of social amenities. Not only these, women as teachers and ethical inculcators in the homes should bring up God-fearing children who will be leaders of tomorrow.

The church as a body and Christians in general have a vital role to play. In spite of the immoral and oppressive measures adopted by the rich people which have created the economic problems of the moment, these same people are found in churches donating generously for the building of churches, occupying big posts in the church, paying their tithes regularly and meeting other financial needs of the church from their ill-gotten wealth. Some of the oppressors and exploiters of our economy are found in the church but in most cases the church is more interested in their fat contributions to church projects than to chastise them.

If Nigeria is to move forward from her present economic, political and social problems, Nigerian Christians must be honest and courageous. The church must place greater emphasis on the morality of its flock than on the money they are contributing. If this is done, Nigeria would enjoy a better economic well-being.

NOTES

1. Crowther M. ***The Story of Nigeria*** (London: Faber and Faber 1978) pg.12

2. Ojiako J. 0 **13 Years of Military Rule** 1966-79 (Lagos: Daily Times) pp 1-5.

3. Ojiako J. 0 1st Four Years of Nigeria Executive Presidency: Success or Failure (Lagos: Daily Times 1983) pg.10.

4. Ezekiel Chapter 3.

5. Asaju D. F. "Pauline Morals in Political Leadership in the Nigerian Context" in D. F. Asaju (Ed) ***Religious Challenges in Nigeria.*** (Lagos: Balifik Educational Publishers 1994) pg.1

6. Lahaye T. ***What Love - Making means to a*** **Woman** (Michigan: Zondervat Press, 1982) pg.37

7. O' Connor in F. Molony ***Women in the N.T*** (Homebush: St. Paul Publications 1981) pg.28 ff.

8. Olajubu 0. "The Role of Women in the N.T. as service to Humanity" in R.Abubakre et al. (eds) Religion and Service to Humanity Nigeria NASR 1993. Pg.142.

JUBILEE AND POLYCARP'S ALTAR OF GOD

Dorcas Akintunde

Introduction

The approach of the millennium is currently eliciting various reactions and responses from across the globe. The city of Assisi, which is the ancestral home of the Franciscan Catholic community, is being given a face-lift.

Similarly, some churches have been organizing prayer meetings, radio and television sponsored programmes etc, while Non-governmental organizations, and other societies organize Seminars, Conferences etc. The various responses exhibited could not, however, be regarded as an act of over-zealousness. This is because the concept of Jubilee is one of hope and the realization of the fact that the so much longed for liberty is quite approaching.

There is no doubt that African countries are similarly longing for the setting-in of the millennium with the hope that it will usher in the anticipated freedom from various economic, social and other related problems which have been ravaging the continent viz. - AIDS, War, Infantile mortality, hunger etc. The continent, like the woman 'bent double' - Luke 13: 10 - 17, is groaning under this burden.

However, at the receiving end of the effect of these various problems are a class of people who form a substantial proportion of the populace - these categories of people are in the words of Polycarp, "an altar of God". In our contemporary society they have the appellation "widows", the term for a woman who has lost her spouse due to those social ills already enumerated or to natural death.

Thus our concern in this work would be to examine the Jubilee proclamation as it affects African Christian widows generally.

Questions for consideration include what has been their portion in the community? What recognition have they been accorded by the society? Are they included in the euphoria of the millennium? How applicable is the concept of Jubilee to them? What are their expectations from religious institutions, individuals and the society at large? Is it possible to reform some cultural demands to suit changing norms, and what effect would it have on the widows if these cultural dictates were reformed?

A glimpse into widows' lives

Mrs. Alibaba (not real name)

I lost my husband on February 14, 1986 in a motor accident when he was just 39.

Our children, three boys, were just 11, 9 and 6 years old. By the time I arrived in the village with the corpse for burial, I shockingly discovered that our house had been shared among his family members. I was questioned for almost two hours and was finally asked to swear an oath with the Bible declaring I had nothing to do with his death. The corpse was washed and I was asked to drink the water used in the process. I refused and told them that the water was poisonous. A sister of his retorted that my refusal was evidence that I killed my husband with my witchcraft. I was left alone without any financial assistance from the in - laws for refusing to marry my husband's younger brother. I stood my ground and I decided to "get married" to my three sons.

Mrs. Otitoloju. (not real name)

... Before the burial ceremony, our belongings were removed and our three cars were sold by my in - laws. All my husband's entitlements which I had been processing were collected before I got to his employer. My brother - in - law who already had two wives and thirteen children was to inherit me, but I vehemently refused. I was finally thrown out together with the schooling and up-keep of the children.

It appears that there may be other parts of the world where widows have unsavory experiences. There have been reports of elderly widowed women being killed for their land in Asia. The experiences of these women portray what it means to be widowed generally. Others include confinement for long periods, shaving of hair and wearing of mourning clothes. Unfortunately, the legal system appears ineffective in dealing with this problem, thus the victim becomes vulnerable to maltreatment and impoverishment. What meaning would Jubilee have for human beings under these obnoxious and inhumane cultural dictates?

Old Testament Concept of Jubilee

Two books in the Old Testament allude to the concept of Jubilee - Lev. 25: 5 - 55 and Isaiah 61: 1 - 6, with the latter as an allusion to the specification in the laws of Moses. Every fiftieth year was to be a year of release marked by four types of release or rest. Debts were to be cancelled, slaves were to be freed, the land was to be granted a year of rest and people who had been forced to sell their family property because of poverty receive it back. The year was to be named 'Year of jubilee', with the literal meaning 'Year of the Ram's Horn[10]- derived from the horn trumpet which was blown to announce its arrival. Jubilee and the Sabbath year's requirements on the part of the people was to portray God's prior action in freeing the Israelites from slavery and hard labor in Egypt. Thus, the imagery of the jubilee - of a royal decree of amnesty, of rest and of liberty as found in Isaiah 61 not only linked to recurring human political and economic activity, but also to the inauguration of the celebration of God's reign. It calls for a new participation in God's reign of justice and peace.

The Jubilee as Proclaimed by Jesus

Luke 4: 18 - 19 records Jesus' reading of Is. 61: 1 -2. Here, the passage as presented by Jesus is a statement of his own commission from God.[13] He had been anointed for a purpose - to announce good news especially to the poor, to heal the captives, recovering of sight to the blind and to set at liberty them that are bruised. (R.S.V). As Tannehill observes, the terms poor, captives, blind and oppressed may have metaphorical range. The poor as he adds refer to all those at the bottom of the economic ladder or scale, who may lack even the basics for survival. Similarly, the captives who are to be released probably include at least three groups - those imprisoned for debts as a result of poverty, those that are with physical ailments as a result of Satan's bondage and lastly those that are oppressed by the devil. Recovery of sight to the blind on the one hand can refer to Jesus' healing ministry and on the other hand it could metaphorically alude to perceiving and sharing in salvation. Thus, the blind may receive their sight in order to turn from darkness to light and from the power of Satan to God. To set at liberty them that are bruised is a remarkable social legislation designed to give the poor a new start. Therefore, Jesus' message as recorded by Luke portrays his concern for the poor which was the motive for the Jubilee proclamation.

Message of Jubilee to the Altar of God

Jesus' message as already enumerated attests to His special interest in the poor, among whom women fall. Thus His message of preaching the gospel to the poor includes the widows. In contemporary society, widows are being pauperized by 'property-grabbing' in-laws. (Mrs. Otitoloju) Some have to resort to working extra hours to cater for their needs coupled with that of the children.

Unfortunately in Africa, the per capital income is very low as is on record that Africa is suffering under chilling destitution characterized by poverty and oppression resulting in constant widening of the gap between the rich and the poor everyday. Thus, one finds these women 'bent double' under the biting economic crunch.

To these 'daughters of Abraham', Jesus' words are apt, '... he hath sent me to heal the broken hearted...' The loss of a loved one, property to relatives, expensive burial rites, dehumanizing cultural rites and the denying of the widow's right to succeed to her husband's property are sufficient basis for grief. The declaration and assumption that the woman herself is a chattel bought and paid for to be inherited by close male members of her husband's family, similarly induce broken heartedness. In like manner, these groups of women have been captives to widowhood rites in the name of religion. These rites vary from community to community. Among the Yoruba, culture demands that she plaits her hair into four throughout the period of widowhood and clothes herself in black attire for as long as the period of mourning lasts ranging between 90 days and 365 days.

Widows in some communities in the Eastern part of the country are subjected to confinement for long periods, shaving of hair, drinking the bath water of the spouse's corpse, eating with unwashed hands and in unwashed plates etc.[18] To them, Jesus says 'He has been appointed with the Holy Spirit to preach deliverance (... where the Spirit of the Lord is, there is liberty 2 Cor. 13:17).

Furthermore, He says ... and recovering of sight to the blind – widows blinded by prolonged crying demand to demonstrate their innocence. They are blinded through the applications of mentholatum, a balm containing menthol and jelly to the eyes to induce tears.

...To set at liberty them that are bruised, - by the whipping they receive from 'daughters of the lineage' in some societies in Nigeria (Imo, Anambra and Cross River), bruised by the leviratic union, which denies them personal freedom. Bruised by the system that robs them of their dignity and bruised internally by the fact that those degrading and inhumane treatments are meted out by people of the same gender. Bruised by the *Kutiti* among the Avatime of Ghana.

To the widows, Jesus' proclamations are apt and soothing. What can we say about the contemporary religious leaders? Are their words soothing to the ears and hearts of widows? Do widows have a portion in the jubilee? Are they to be left in the cold hands of customary rites for ever? What have been the religious institutions' responses to their plight? Do men undergo such demanding and demeaning rites?

RELIGIOUS INSTITUTIONS AND WIDOWS

Oduyoye observes that 'rites for widowers tend not to be exotic or as lurid, demanding and demeaning as widows' rites.' In essence, widowers are not bound to adhere to some of these cultural dictates. Thus, they could remarry as soon as possible and the rules of confiriement are not binding on widowers, as it is believed that they need to move around to cater for the children, and possibly, other wives too.

Religious institutions, like the society they mirrored, have not succeeded in alleviating the problems of widows. The church for example, has failed to follow the example of Jesus who on several occasions associated with them and 'bids their sorrows cease'. The Old Testament is also replete with how religious leaders related with them, e.g., Elijah and the Shunnamite Widow, the widow of Zarephat, etc. These religious leaders (Prophets and Jesus) still challenge us today to stretch out humanitarian hands to this class of people. What have we done about their cries against these demeaning and obnoxious cultural practices? Have we devised enough strategies in order to support them economically, spiritually and otherwise? Have we given them enough recognition in our associations? What can men/husbands do to liberate their wives, sisters and daughters from these oppressive systems? Should women, widows, be allowed to suffer unjustly? If the church is 'the body of Christ' on earth, and Christ has come with the jubilee proclamation, will He be delighted that a part of His body is left to suffer unjustly by His representatives on earth?

THE WAY FORWARD

Women need to roll the wheel of progress themselves. Official records as it pertains to next of kin both at the bank and with the employer need to be reviewed as soon as persons get married. This is because many in- laws show up to collect entitlements, thus leaving the widow to wallow in poverty. Women in the church could assist the widows not only in being sympathetic, but materially as Dorcas did. That her service was to the widows in Acts. 9:39, indicates a specialized or on - going ministry, and not just an occasional good deed to friends or neighbours. The story of Ruth and Naomi points to an understanding of how women should be responsible for looking after themselves, particularly in relation to many rituals that are detrimental to women's well-being. In this wise, the concerned sisters could organize seminars, workshops, conferences, aimed at demystifying some of the practices which oppress, while those which enhance the communal nature of Africans, and are aimed at incorporating the widows back into the society could be encouraged. Custom - laden ladies should be conscientized to the fact that culture is dynamic as it evolves and changes with time.

Men could similarly help in solving parts of the problems of property grabbing by buying things jointly with their wives and securing official records as evidence. This will effectively keep greedy relatives at bay.

In like manner, there is the need for women's pressure groups to bring pressure to bear on the government of the day to take legislative measures to incorporate CEDAW24 (Convention of the Elimination of All Forms of Discrimination Against Women) into our domestic laws in parts of Africa where this has not been implemented. Pressure should also be brought to bear on the government to ensure full respect, protection and fulfillment of the exercise and enjoyment of human rights and fundamental freedom of women on a basis of equality with men, especially along the line of the provisions of CEDAW.

Committee Against Torture (CAT) should also be established to eradicate some of the practices that are detrimental to health. We realized that some of these laws exist in theory only. In dealing with human lives, they should become pragmatic. Reformation and implementation of laws that ensure the inheritance and citizenship rights of girls, women and widows, are suggested. Government also needs to develop infrastructure to provide social, economic and educational opportunities for all women as this would make for economic independence.

Religious institutions need to conscientize and educate men on the need to involve their wives in their financial transactions and what becomes of the wives and children after death. Groups of religious women could be organized to educate women frequently in order to alert them of their rights and the need to 'fight' for these rights.

The role of the mass media, both print and electronic, could not be overemphasized. Portraits of widows in their mourning moods and deplorable health situations undergone during the period of widowhood should be displayed and periodically to conscientize the populace and especially the men. This we believe, would lead them to ask, would I want my wife, my daughter, my sister or my children to undergo these rituals? Would they, in this condition, be able to sing:

Blow ye the trumpet blow,

The gladly solemn sound,

Let all the nations know,

To earth's remotest bound,

The Year of Jubilee is come ...

Notes

1. Part of the statement made by Sr. Nasimiyu Wasike, A Roman Catholic Rev. Sr. at the Conference organized by the Circle of Concerned African Women Theologian in Accra - Ghana, between Oct. 5 - 10, 1999.

2. Radio and Television Stations in Nigeria relay religious - sponsored programme. For example, the Oyo State Broadcasting Corporation aired such programmes on Sunday l0th Oct., 1999 at 5. 45p.m.

3. One of such was organized by the Concerned African Women Theologian, tagged African Women Theologian and Jubilee 2000, between 5th Oct. – 10th Oct., 1999.

4. Abogunrin S. 0. 'Religion And Democracy in Nigeria' in *ORITA, Ibadan Journal of Religious Studies,* Vol. XXXI/ 1 - 2, June & Dec. 1999, pp. 1 - 18.

5. Nadia M. Lahutsky, 'Widows' in *Dictionary of Feminist Theology* (eds.) Letty M. Russell & Shannon Clarkson. Westminster John Knox Press, 1996: pp. 314 -315. Polycarp also urges them to pray ceaselessly for the church.

6. The report was by Nike Sotade in: *The Guardian* (Nigerian Newspaper), Wednesday, June 4,1997, p. 32.

7. Ibid.

8. Women Envision: A Publication of Isis International, March, 1998, no. 55, p. 3.

9. Sharon Ringe, Luke. Westminster John Knox Press, Louisville, Kentucky, 1995,p.68ff.

10. Barry Webb. *The Message of Isaiah.* Inter Varsity Press, England, 1996, p.234.

11. Sharon Ringe. *Op.cit.* p.68.

12. Tannehill Robert C. *Luke.* Abingdon Press, Nashville, 1996, p. 91.

13. Ibid. p. 91.

14. Ibid. p. 91.

15. Matthew Theuri, 'Poverty in Africa' in *Theology of Reconstruction: Exploratory Essays.* (eds.) Mary Getui & Emmanuel Obeng. Acton Publishers, Nairobi, Kenya, 1999, pp. 230 -242.

16. The leviratic union to some theologians - Michael Kirwen - exists to uphold and prolong marriages as it is understood in African societies, whereas to some others, (Paul Kalanda), it is illicit. He argues that a wife may be 'wife' of the family as a whole, but she still remains primarily wife of an individual member of the family, thus other men in the family are denied sexual and domestic rights over her.

17. The writer is an indigene of that part of Nigeria.

18. Theresa Akumadu. *Beasts of Burden: A Study of Women's Legal Status and Reproductive Health Rights in Nigeria.* A Pub. Of The Women's Rights Project, C.L.O. Lagos Nigeria, 1998. P. 61.

19. Ganusah Rebecca 'Widowhood Beliefs and Practices of the Avatime' in Amoah Elizabeth (ed.) *Mere God Reigns: Reflection of Women in*

God's World. Sam-Wood's Ltd., Accra - North, Ghana, 1997. Pp. 135 -158.

20. Oduyoye Mercy, quoting Ajisafe Moore: *The Laws and Customs of the Yoruba People.* Abeokuta, Nigeria, n.d. p. 75.

21. From oral interview with some colleagues at the University of Ibadan. It was gathered that some societies provide 'alternative' wife before the widowers could remarry. This was to prevent the wife's ghost from luring the man into relationship.

22. Potgieter Sharon 'Church Praxis and Women Who Remained Within The Church' in *Groaning in Faith. African Women in the Household of God. K* Musimbi & Njoroge N. (eds.) Acton Pub. Nairobi, Kenya, 1996. Pp. 16 -22.

23. Ben Witherington; *Women in the Earliest Churches.* C.U.P. Britain, 1988. P. 87ff.

24. Eze Onyekpere (ed.) *Manual on Gender Specific Rights Litigation And Protection Strategies,* Lagos, Nigeria, 1998, pp. 47 - 58.

25. Articles 2,10,12, and 16 of CEDAW deal with the rights to freedom from discrimination and equality of the sexes, the right to education, the right to health and the right to equality in marriage and in the family respectively. *Ibid.*

26. *Ibid.* p. 58.

27. Selected from Compilation of Songs by S. 0. Folahan. *Soul Moving Hymns and Choruses,* Dec. 1998, Appendices No. 4.

The Kayayolization of Muslim Girls; Jubilee and After

Rabiatu Ammah

Introduction

The debt crisis in African countries has led many to call for the cancellation of these by the creditors. Thus people have called for a Jubilee. What really does this mean especially to the children on the streets of Accra? How will cancellation of debt affect the standard of living of the child? As a Muslim woman, although the "Jubilee" has no direct equivalent in Islam, it is still relevant because the underlying principles are equally Islamic and they purport to bring about social equality and honoring the dignity of all human beings.

As a Muslim woman, Jubilee 2000 is relevant to me, first, because of marginalization and because poverty affects me. More importantly, it must not only be honored but women must get involved in strategizing for the next millennium. They must be part and parcel of the process that should lead to transformation of the situation in Ghana in general and the world as a whole. Women should be involved if they are to move to the center and bring about the much-needed transformation. The involvement of women is therefore not only crucial but also essential.

However in honoring the Jubilee, women and especially Muslim women should address certain critical issues if the Jubilee should be meaningful.

These are:

- Where are we?
- Where do we hope to be?
- How do we get there?
- How do we maintain the position and move on?

It would seem that these are management or marketing questions. However as women who have been marginalized, these questions are critical areas of concern. Until and unless these areas are addressed the debt cancellation and the whole Jubilee concept would mean nothing.

In this paper I shall try to examine the underlying principles of the Jubilee concept in Islam, then the paper will discuss the situation of the street children especially the porter girls (kayayo) and finally make recommendation as to how the Jubilee can impact the Ghanaian community and trickle down to them. Even more critical, how to get them involved in this struggle for transformation.

Jubilee and Islam

There is no exact equivalent of Jubilee in the Islamic tradition. However there are principles and teachings, which point to this. The essence of the Jubilee can also be found in the Quran and Sunna, the scriptures upon which the religion is based. If Jubilee is about stock taking and forgiveness, then the Muslim fasting during the month of Ramadan teaches this. A Muslim is obliged to abstain from food and drink, sexual intercourse and smoking from dawn to dusk for a period of 29 or 30 davs. This exercise which takes place during the month of Ramadan is ordained for Muslims with the aim of learning piety and self-restraint. As a Muslim, the exercise teaches amongst others, principles, brotherly love, sympathy and forgiveness. Muslims learn to share, give, love, and to show mercy on all creatures of God. This month is one of stock taking, as it provides Muslims with time to strategize about how to improve their spiritual lives. Immediately after the Ramadan, the Muslim is tested by being asked to give out *the Sakat UL* Fitr to the poor. This shows whether Muslims have really inculcated the moral values that are expected of them.

Stock-taking is expected to lead to transformation, as every year brings the annual pilgrimage to Mecca. At Hajj the Thram blurs the social distinctions and teaches that before God all are equal. The ritual associated with Hajj teaches the principle of dignity of human being and social equality.

In yet another pillar of Islam, the Sakat is instituted for Muslims to be able to be their brothers and sisters' keeper. Through the Sakat the Muslim is told not only to forgive the debt but also to pay the debt of a Muslim. Actually the Sakat is instituted so that the debt is not incurred at all. This system which is crucial for the achievement of social equality and justice is one issue that will be discussed later.

The five pillars of Islam are all geared towards acknowledging the dignity and worth of human-beings who are khalifas or representatives of God on earth. Thus, humans are obliged to imitate the qualities of God on earth. The concept of mercy, love and forgiveness are therefore relevant to our discussion.

In Islam God is al-Gafiir and noted to be the all Forgiving. God forgives our sins if we repent sincerely and follow the right path. Consequently God shows mercy and forgives us because we are fallible. However there is the *proviso* that forgiveness will only come after sincere repentance. God therefore forgives and encourages Muslims to also forgive and show mercy to other Muslims. According to a hadith of the Prophet, during the month of Ramadan God is so merciful that the doors of hell are closed.

This forgiveness of sins was put into practice after the conquest of Makka when the Prophet granted amnesty to the Polytheists who had persecuted and meted out injustice to him and his fellow Muslims. Again in his farewell sermon, the Prophet said, among other things, that:

- right to homicide should be waived
- interest on loans should be waived
- love, brotherhood and justice should be practised
- dignity of the human being should be acknowledged and that all human beings are one.

Within Islamic tradition, there are underlying principles which address the social equality of human beings, honoring the identity of all and taking care of the poor. Yet these principles which are found in most religious traditions do not mean much in the Ghanaian society. This is reflected in the lives of the street children especially the *kayayee.*

Situation of street children

Walking around the streets of Accra, one is struck by the number of children ranging from as young as 6 years to 20 years, hawking all sorts of wares. These children, when interviewed, had a variety of reasons for being there. Yet the main reason is that of poverty. They have to hawk to be able to fend for themselves. The usual reason one hears is that "my parents cannot look after me so I dropped out of school." Some also say that they could not continue with the Junior Secondary School and have thus come down to Accra to find ways of earning a living. They render services and are patronized by many on the streets. However, for some time now, the Accra Metropolitan Authority personnel harass the children because they are considered to be:

- too many on the streets
- a security hazard
- breaking the law by hawking
- endangering their lives.

The sanctions range from instant caning to confiscation of their wares. I witnessed a boy of about 13 being caned for selling onions on the pavement at Makola and it raised several questions. Is this boy really ready to face the next millennium? Will this talk about jubilee mean anything to him? Should he be caned for trying to make a living? Who has created the situation in which he finds himself?

Much as the situation of the street children is pathetic, that of the *kayayoo* is even worse and more relevant to me because I am a Muslim. A visit to any market in the metropolis reveals that a lot of teenage girls act as 'porter girls.' They usually have names like Amina, Fati, Sala and Rabiatu. This presupposes that they are Muslims and come from Muslim families or have Muslim backgrounds. Most of these girls, ranging between the ages of 12-22 have trekked from mainly the northern regions of Ghana to Accra. The *kayayee* carry loads for a fee. They therefore offer valuable services to women and should be commended.

The main reason why these girls are performing these jobs, however menial it may be, is to be able to earn a living. According to most of them, they come from poor families. Most of them have very little education if at all, or dropped out of school because their parents could not afford the financial resources needed to see them through. According to some of them, they dropped out of school so that their brothers could be given the opportunity of getting the education that could be afforded. Thus some of them have come to the cities to make some money to send home for their brothers to be educated. The reality of the situation is that poverty has affected the *kayayoo* and driven her into the streets to earn a living. Yet, the *kayayoo* is not only exploited but also faces a lot of hazards.

One of such is security. Due to the fact that the *kayayoo* is already poor, and has very little resources, she has no proper place of habitation. She cannot rent a room and is forced to sleep in the open in the market. She is subjected to the hazards of the weather and therefore prone to diseases and sicknesses.

Another problem that the kayayoo is subjected to is rape and sexual abuse. There have been several incidents where babies have been dropped into rubbish pits and KVIPs at Agbogbloshie markets and the suspects have been the *kayayee.* Since they have very little security and privacy, they are sometimes sexually abused and violence is meted out to them. When the children are born, most of the time without pre-natal care, they are also bred on the streets. These children who are born to children will have the same life to lead if nothing is drastically done to improve the situation for the future generation.

The situation of the kayayoo and the process of kayayolization is an issue that has to be addressed by Muslim women especially if the underlying reason for this inhuman condition is poverty. What has led to it? How can poverty and the problems associated with it be alleviated in the Muslim community? These are some of the issues to which the paper now addresses.

Historical Context

It is not by accident that *the kayayoo* finds herself in this predicament. As a result of the attitude of Muslims to the colonial systems of education, which was rightly or wrongly equated with Christianity, many Muslims were not sent to school. Muslims simply saw the secular education as another avenue for the Christians to evangelize. And this really took place in several missionary schools. Children were indoctrinated and converted. They had to change their names from Rabiatu to Ruth before they could be accepted. This policy of proselytization therefore, discouraged Muslims from going to school. The consequences of the inability or refusal to have secular education where Muslims could be taught skills and vocation were that it cost them a lot. They were pushed to the margins and could not hold important official positions. Thus they could not make their voices to be heard where it mattered. The late Dr Kwame Nkrumah proposed a fee-free education especially for the Northern regions of the country, to redress the imbalance. Economically therefore, Muslims are found at the bottom of the social economic ladder in Ghana. Although the situation is changing the harm has already been done to a whole generation of Muslim men and women.

Consequently, in Ghana today, people have negative images and stereotyped ideas about Muslims in general and the women in particular. They are thought of as being illiterate and ignorant. As I dropped off my aunt, a boy of barely ten stared at me. I therefore demanded why he was staring and especially when he kept saying, "As for this, I haven't seen some before." "What haven't you seen some before? Is it the woman driving or the woman wearing *mayafi* and driving?" "The latter." He replied.

Initially I thought it was funny but soon realized the seriousness of it when I asked why the boy should have such an attitude and mentality about me. Is driving incompatible with my religion? How did he come about this image? Whatever the answers are the fact remains that his impression is not an isolated case. It is also not surprising since Muslim women are noted to be *waakye* sellers, hawkers of groundnuts, fula and *koko* sellers. The phenomenon of the *kayayoo* is not surprising since it is indicative of a cycle of poverty.

Avenues for change

Much as the *kayayoo* is on the margin, it is just one example of how poverty has adversely affected the lives of people. This is not to say that only Muslim women are poor as is exaggerated by many Muslims. They hammer on their poor economic standing and assert that for example, the recent introduction of the user fees will affect them most. The fact is that so many of the children in the streets are poor but are not necessarily Muslim. How then can the Jubilee ameliorate the condition of the Muslim women and the *kayayee?*

The critical question that must be considered is, "Will the cancellation of the debt mean anything to the *kayayoo?* This reminds me of a conversation I had with my son who asked; the year 2000 will the world change? Will the sky become red? So why is everybody talking about Y2K? nothing is going to change." I am tempted to say again that the Jubilee will not mean anything to the *kayayoo* if certain fundamental changes do not take place. It is assumed by some that if the debts are cancelled poverty will be miraculously alleviated and the standard of living will improve. It seems that if the debt is cancelled and people are not encouraged to be self-sufficient but always reliant on others, very little will be achieved. If the debt is cancelled but the benefits that accrue from it do not trickle down to the *kayayoo and* her children nothing would be achieved. The kayayoo must be well established in life with working tools so that she can render better services to the nation. The vocation must be professionalized so as to give her some form of security and protection. Although probably very little can be done for the kayayoo presently to radically change her status, it could be a long-term project that would benefit and guarantee that her children do not end up like her.

But as a Muslim woman I also feel that for Muslims to talk about marginalization and do nothing consciously about it is unIslamic. This is basic to self development. The Muslim woman must therefore focus on the education of her children and make sure that the female children are not removed from school. They must appreciate the value of education. Again the Muslims must get their priorities right. It is important to note that privatization is a cardinal element for success. Muslims must be able to determine the priority areas. For example, muslim women spend a lot of time and energy on *awule, Sunna anadua* (marriage, out-dooring and funerals). Women especially show lots of affluence and display such vanity that sometimes one wonders whether Muslims are as poor as they claim to be. It is common to see a Muslim woman pile up bowls, cups, plates and soap in a cupboard and yet is unable to afford an exercise book for a child to go to school.

The unnecessary waste of money on expensive dressing especially at the two *eids* by the women of Zabon, Zongo and Nima are all signs of misplaced priorities and social injustices. In this regard, efforts should be made to conscientize women to change their attitude towards acts that lead to poverty. After all it is unIslamic to be affluent whilst some suffer.

Another way by which the Muslim woman, and by extension the *kayayoo* can benefit is through the Zakat Fund. The zakat is one of the means by which the gap between the rich and the poor is bridged. Thus the *kayayoo* can be helped if the fund is well instituted and managed. However, due to the inability of the Muslims to work out the fund, zealous Muslims are not willing to contribute to the Zakat Fund which can be used to institute vocational schools to train girls to render better services and help alleviate poverty. The fund is of great importance to the community at large and must be established to help bring about social equality and justice.

Conclusion

The Kayayoo on the street will welcome Jubilee 2000 and look forward to some transformation and ease in her life. All women will. However there must be right structures to help achieve the aim and purpose of the Jubilee. This can only be done by human beings when they make conscious efforts to change and amend their ways. After all people create the structures, images are created by people. People decide to forgive and cancel. It is the same people who decide to find alternative and better ways of doing things. In the Quantico or Islamic tradition "Allah will not change a people until they change themselves." If we all individually, nationally and globally amend our ways, the debt cancellation will impact and bring about the underlying principles of the jubilee-social equality, acknowledging the dignity of human beings and the implementation of justice.

Verbal abuse against women

Christina Landman

Introduction

The Circle of African Women Theologians is ten years old. It was convoked at a meeting in Accra, Ghana, held from September 24 to October 2 in 1989.

From the very beginning, the publications of this Circle dealt with the issue of abuse. These publications dealt mainly with three kinds of abuse and they did so in a very sophisticated and innovative way, if I may say. The three types of abuse most popular in African women's theologies are:

Cultural abuse. This is abuse inflicted on women by culture, rituals and the ways in which women's sexuality is prescribed to them.

Sexual abuse. Here reference, is mainly to rape, both inside and outside of marrirage

Domestic violence. This deals mainly with physical abuse inside personal relationship

Today I want to plead with you that we shall introduce another type of abuse into our Research because of the fact that it is so widespread. This is *verbal abuse.* In South Africa a new law on abuse is in the making which will come into effect on 15 December this year. This law addresses all kinds of abuse against women and make them punishable. What is amazing and liberating about this law is that it acknowledges verbal and emotional abuse as criminal offenses.

Women and verbal abuse

Definition: Verbal abuse is the use of words with the intention to hurt, not allowing the abused any words.

Field of study

The research for this study is part of a larger project which interviews blackand and white South African women, socio-economically from the upper middle class, who are engaged in or divorced from heterosexual relationships. This paper deals with the experiences of ten white, black and colored women, half of them married and half divorced. They were from different age groups.

They were chosen for the similarity in their experiences of verbal abuse. Their color made little difference to these experiences.

Faces of verbal abuse

Wherever verbal abuse occurs, the husband (or ex-husband in the memories of the divorced) usually, if not always, targets those areas in the wife's life which traditionally are known as women's territory, areas in which women still today want to perform.

Buying the Groceries

The women interviewed were either not allowed to work outside the house, or they were made to pay their salaries into their husbands' accounts. In all the cases the women were not allowed to know how much their husbands earned.

Claudine (38) told me that her husband never gave her any allowance. He went with her to buy the groceries because, he said, she would just waste his money. She did needlework to buy basic things for herself and her two small daughters. After 12 years of marriage she is now divorced. Before her marriage she was a bookkeeper, but because of a lack of career experience, she is now a counter clerk at a bank. She cannot survive on her salary and borrows money from her brother. Since he has forced her to sleep with him since primary school, one only wonders what these loans will cost her.

Chris (50) has been a nurse but her husband forced her to leave her job. However, he does not want to support her. He buys the groceries and she has to ask him money even to buy the daily bread. When he found out that she was earning money through selling homemade things, he forced her to give half of her income to him and use the other half to buy household goods.

Charmaine (28) was found in a house for poor people after she had fled from home. After her husband had lost money in a property deal, he insisted on buying the groceries. To assert his power and his lost esteem, he refused to buy her the things she personally needed, like shampoo. Later he even refused to buy her toilet paper. He would also buy chips and sweets instead of fresh produce, which she preferred, and counted down for her little heap of chips and sweets with that of the children.

Maria (30) was physically abused by her husband after taking money from his purse. He never gave her any money and she needed money for the children. She then asked me whether I thought she had sinned.

In all these cases, the woman was not permitted to own anything, she was treated as a child and told that she deserved this because she was financially unreliable. Buying groceries then became a battle-ground in the relationship, with the husband keeping necessary household goods from the wife as a way of exercising power over her. These women simply do not have the money to leave the relationship and if they attempt it, they indeed suffer financially, to a point of being unable to survive.

Cooking and housekeeping

The house was never clean enough, tells Claudia, and he always criticized my food. He would leave the table in the middle of the dinner and go dining with his girl friend.

My husband bought a couch for the living room. I then made little cloths to protect it, but he cut them up, tells Christine. I am not allowed to work outside the house, but inside, I may also not do anything. Everything belongs to him.

Looks and Sex

My husband does not give me money to have my hair cut and then makes hurting remarks about my appearance. Once my mother gave me a new dress and he tore it up. Thus tells Daniella.

All the women interviewed told me that their (ex) husbands harrassed them with the words that sex was inadequate with them and that they needed other women. The women themselves were not allowed to greet the neighbour or speak on the phone when a man called. All of them were accused of having affairs while their husbands' affairs were confirmed.

The Children

One day, tells Marilyn, I could not take his abuse anymore I just broke down. They took me to the hospital. My husband then came there with two letters. The one was to say that he was not going to pay for the hospital costs (we did not have medical aid then because he had lost his business. The other was to say that I must keep away from the children. I was in such a state I did not know what I was signing. I signed away my children.

My ex-husband used to call me every night to tell me what a hopeless mother I was, tells Claudine. I was not allowed to go out, even though we were divorced. I could only take the children to school outings and even then we had to be back before eight. If he'd tailed and we were not there, there was big trouble. Eventually I broke down. An hour after I was taken up in hospital and was still under sedation, he called to say that he was not going to pay for this (although I was still on his medical scheme). He then used this incident (that is, my breaking down) to take the children away from me. I was not fit to defend myself. I was found an unfit mother by the court, although I spent my life to bring them up and was not allowed to work outside the house.

Charmaine's family brought her to a mental clinic after she fled home with no money and was missing for three days. While she was in the clinic her husband sold all her clothes and gave away her dog, which was the only living thing still of value to her.

All the divorced women interviewed lost their children. Those remaining in marriage do so because of the threat that they will not be allowed to keep the children. One day I put my children on the bus to go to my mother. We all had had enough. My husband had hit my daughter the previous day so badly that the school called and said that she had bleeding wounds. When the bus stopped near my mother's house, my husband pulled in behind in the bus. He said that I could go, he did not care, but that the children would never go with me. I went back. I do not know why he wanted the children; he did not even seem to like them.

Frustrations of the Research

As a researcher I often wept with these women when they told me their stories. I also wept because I was not able to record the full extent of the verbal abuse committed against them. There are three reasons for this:

- The women were not able to tell me the actual words, which hurt them. They told me the circumstances leading to them but not the words themselves. I am quite sure that they knew them very well, but retelling was humiliating. This points to the extent of the damage done by verbal abuse.

- Retelling their stories of hurt, even though they left out the actual words said to them, retraumatised the women. After a woman has told me her story, I usually try to stay the night, even for three or four days, because she would surely get nightmares during this time. Even though I try to guide the story towards a healing end, the experience of telling her story easily turns into a trauma for the woman.

- What is particularly heart breaking for me while doing this research, is the fact that the women involved were quite allergic to any gender talk which would try to give them insight into their situation. They would not accept that a genderised power game was the cause of their pain. They would blame themselves for the situation, evaluating themselves according to the traditional expectations for women. Or they would ask me why God is punishing them unrightfully.

For me as a researcher it was frightful to see how stereotypical the women's views were, not only of themselves as women, but also of their husbands. Their heartbrokenness was situated in the fact that their husbands did not conform to their idea of what a good husband is.

Typical behavior of a verbally abused woman

- There is no doubt that verbal abuse has a profound influence on a woman's life. The women interviewed all had minor or major breakdowns, all of them more than once. The divorced ones amongst them were all still wetting their beds after the verbal abuse of the divorce.

- All of the women had a poor self-image. They were constantly making sneering remarks about themselves. I asked one of the women to count how many times a day she said something nasty about herself - and she counted 42 for that particular day.

- All these women were yearning to change their bodies to conform to the stereotype of the sexy blonde. Having a beautiful body brings new hope, they all believe. Annette, for instance, borrowed money from the bank (she earns only R1000 per month after 24 years of a career less marriage) to have her breasts reduced, to get injections to lose weight, to have her teeth redone, and to have herself sewn up below to give a man as much pleasure as possible.

- All the women interviewed were looking for religious answers to their predicament.

Most of them believed that God was punishing them. And if He was not punishing them, they wanted to know why He was 'not able to prevent this from happening. In all of these God is seen as the God of the *status quo* who favors the politics of domestication.

The divorced women believed that God hated divorce and that they should not have divorced their husbands even though he was verbally abusing them and had a steady girlfriend.

Simultaneously most of them also wanted to know why God was not punishing the man. Annette marked all the places in the Bible where God condemned adultery. She sent them to her ex-husband and his new wife with the message that he could still turn around and come back before the judgment of God would get at him.

All the divorced women, incidentally, were unable to enter into new relationships after their divorce and bemoaned their divorces, although they were initiated by themselves.

Finally the women consoled themselves with the thought that their tribulations were sent by God to make them stronger.

A Theology of Safety

From the above it is clear that women need a theology to guard their safety.

What would such a theology of safety look like?

Renaming the sacred: *Renaming God*

In renaming God, a women's theology of safety will take at least two roads:

This theology will replace male references to God which imply hierarchical authority, such as Father and King, with references to God as Protector and Caretaker.

However, this theology does not want to suggest that God protects us while expecting from us to remain passive. God also liberates people to look after and fight for themselves. God, the Protector, therefore always implies God the Liberator.

Reclaiming Christ

A theology of safety needs to rethink the emphasis theology in the past has placed on Christ's suffering. Women who are being abused should not be confronted with Christ the Sufferer, but Christ the Survivor, the One who has survived death and has risen to new life. Christ the Victim should be reclaimed as Christ the Survivor. For too long women have thought that their role in society was that of self-sacrifice and undeserving servanthood.

A theology of safety wants to teach women that their first moral and religious responsibility is to their own safety, also from verbal abuse, and to that of their children.

Re-experiencing the Spirit

In order to escape from the pain of (verbal) abuse, and because verbal abuse is usually directed towards their sexuality and womanhood, abused women often entertain some strange, or rather estranging, ideas about their bodies. They believe that through bodily suffering, for instance through anorexia, they would become more acceptable to the abuser. Or they believe that they suffer abuse as punishment for something their souls are responsible for.

However, a theology of safety wishes to ensure women that the Spirit of God resides in them, making them worthy as human beings.

Redefining our Neighbour

Anthropology: Rediscovering women as human beings

Three points are of importance here:

- A theology of safety rejects an anthropology which teaches women to be selfless and self-negating to a point where they do not put their safety first.
- A women's theology of safety acknowledges a woman's right to her own identity. A woman has a right to have an identity separate from that of her husband, her parents, or her children.
- Women theologians are concerned about the many systems and values of society which make women feel guilty when they do not conform to the ideals of selflessness and self-negation.

In short, a theology of safety emphasizes women's identity and self worth, thereby replacing the notions of dependence and guilt, which have ruled the lives of many women in the past and still put them in a vulnerable position as far as abuse is concerned.

Ecclesiology: Redefining women's place in the church

A theology of safety supports the idea of *a just peace church.* This means that women should be re-instated in the church as office bearers as they were in the early church. However, the wrongs done to women in the past by churches excluding them from fully participating in church life on all levels should first be dealt with. Only then can there *be just peace* in the church.

Ecology: Rediscovering women as healers of the earth

A theology of safety wants to empower women to put their own safety first. However, it does not want to suppress women's ability to care for others, especially for the co-abused. Nature falls into this category of the co-abused and a theology of safety encourages women to engage, in spite of and driven by their own pain, in healing the earth.

Revoicing Ourselves

A new voice in Ethics

A theology of safety addresses quite a few ethical issues amongst which are the following

- *The problem of premature forgiveness.* A theology of safety reminds a woman of her ethical right not to forgive her abuser before he has changed his behavior. Forgiveness cannot even be discussed before the abused woman is safe.

- *The problem of breaking the covenant of marriage.* May an abused woman leave a marriage and thus break the covenant of marriage? Is it ethically correct for her not to forgive an abuser who does not intend changing his behavior and get a divorce? A theology of safety points out that when a woman leaves a relationship because of battering, it is not she who has broken the covenant of marriage, but the abuser. The marriage covenant does not confer the power to abuse a partner.

A new voice in Politics

A theology of safety wants to activate three institutions to actively work towards assuring women

- T*he church,* to conscientise Christians towards women's safety.

- *Society,* to create a safe space for women in which to live, work and relax; and
- *The state,* to guard women through legislation.

A new voice on sexuality,

A theology of sexuality wants to educate the public in the following fields:

- Women should be taught to take control over their self-image.
- Societies should be taught to acknowledge the integrity of women.
- Women and men should be taught to sort out the conflict between women's emotional needs, men's needs and women's safety needs.

In conclusion

- *The question of theodicy.* The question of theodicy asks: Where is God when I suffer? Abused women usually give one of two answers to this question: they are either convinced that God has abandoned them or they believe that God is punishing them for something, A theology of safety answers this question in the following way: The abused woman is reminded that the abuser has chosen to batter. It is important that the woman should understand that she is not abused by God but by a man who has abused and is abusing her not because he cannot help it, but because he has chosen to do so. There is nothing transcendental about being abused; it is a human problem which needs to and can be solved. The abused woman is reminded that God is her God too, and that she may empower herself through God against her abuser.

In South Africa, parliament is in the process of accepting legislation which makes verbal abuse illegal. It is our job to make it practical and theologically viable for women to stand up against this type of abuse.

March 16, 1999.

5

RELATED PAPERS

'THE IMPACT OF JUBILEE ON OUR LIVES'

Amba Oduyoye

Jubilee is a biblical term, a Judaeo-Christian concept that has gone into the English language for the celebration of significant anniversaries, silver jubilee, Golden jubilee, Platinum jubilee. These are all anniversaries during which we would like to blow our horns. For truly jubilee comes from a word meaning, a horn. The Hebrew people made their horns from the horns off a ram's head. Asante *ahemfo* have several horns usually from elephant tusks and they are blown together with drums to herald the coming of *ahemfo* and *ahemmaa.* Jubil is a ram's horn and to jubilate is to blow your own horn. Our subject however seems to require us to deal with a specific year of jubilee. So I imagine we would like to make connections with the **'Jubilee 2000'** campaign that is a movement to get the cancellation of the debts owed to the rich countries by the poor countries of our global community. But first let us go to the Christian roots to ask the question on, "what impact does the concept of jubilee have on our lives?"

JUBILEE IN HEBREW SCRIPTURES

We remember how the Hebrew people circled the walls of Jericho six times in six days, blew the horn on the 7th day and saw the walls tumbling down. (Joshua 6:1-20). The priest blew the *mmenson* - and great was the jubilation as the walls of Jericho collapsed. The Jubilee 2000 movement wants a march that will make the wall that barricade the rich fall down so that the resources of God's earth might be for all God's people and not just for God's rich people. This concept of Jubilee 2000 connotes storming the garrisons of powers that have become obstacles to Africa's march towards human development. What to note here is that the People of Israel were not just sitting and waiting for Jericho to be delivered into their hands, they were marching. Priests and all were on the move obeying the instructions of God as to how to achieve their aim. Many of us, I dare say, do not even know that we are in debt or that there is injustice involved in our being labeled debtors and that those who have led us into the slavery of debt should atone for their sins of exploitation and make reparations. Sounding of the *mmen* that has to do with ridding a community of sins including exploitation of others is found in Lev. 25 after the account of the Day of Atonement held on the 10th day of the 7th month.

THE YEAR OF JUBILEE

The number seven has a very significant place in Hebrew spirituality. God created the universe in six days and rested on the seventh. It became the Sabbath rest. God instructed Moses to tell the children of Israel to keep the Sabbath rest. Sow your fields for six years and then let the field rest on the seventh.

When you have had 7x7 years then "declare the 50th year sacred and proclaim the liberation of all the land. This is to be a jubilee year for you," it shall be a holy year.

- Each of you will return to the ancestral home
- Do no wrong in trading- Land must not be sold in perpetuity. The right of redemption must be honored.
- Support those who fall on hard times.

The jubilee deals with the cancellation of debts, freeing of slaves, environmental justice (let the land rest) redemption of family property. To begin this work of reparation and repair the Ram's Horn is blown.

The practice recalls how Israel was given a new lease of life from the days of slavery in Egypt. The sound of the Jubilee horn marks a new beginning for all and Isaiah expounds this vision in the third section of that book.

Isaiah 61

The prophet sees himself as sent by God to stimulate the practice of the tenets of Jubilee. Very often commentators remind us that the year of the Jubilee was never observed, as it should be in Israel. It remained on the Torah as a challenge to national morality. To-day it has come down to us to teach us compassion and urge us to demand justice from the rich whose life-styles are supported by the poor. The Hebrew people paid lip service to it as the political and economic changes did not allow such a social consciousness to operate. Nevertheless, all the biblical prophets kept reminding Israel of aspects of this demand from God. Isaiah announced:

"The spirit of the Lord Yahweh has been given to me, for Yahweh has anointed me. He has sent me to bring good news to the poor to bind up hearts that are broken, to proclaim liberty to captives, freedom to those in prison, comfort those who mourn. They will build the ancient ruins. The divine spirit is one that binds up the wounded and restores integrity where brokenness has taken hold of people and their communities. Hence we pray the spirit of God to direct both us and our "creditors".Yahweh loves justice, hates robbery, and all that is wrong. Therefore "As the earth makes fresh things grow, as a garden makes seeds spring up so will the Lord Yahweh make both integrity and praise spring up in the sight of the nations" (excerpts from verse one to eleven.)

All this is of course contingent upon heeding the sound of the horn that calls for release of the captives. When Jesus picked up the Book of Isaiah in His home synagogue He had to remind them of the Year of the Lord, the day of vengeance of God. The day on which God will ensure that the meek shall inherit the earth.

The Gospel According to Luke

Luke's gospel is a demonstration of how Jesus lived the demands of Jubilee. When Luke recorded the Nazareth event he added that on the day of God's favour there will be "recovery of sight to the blind,"

This is what "Jubilee 2000" is all about. The Southern hemisphere which is known as the Third World is witnessing the effect of 10 jubilee years of exploitation by Europeans and people of European descent. These are areas of the world now said to be in debt. Those who were blind to this process of exploitation have to have their eyes opened, so no one can plead ignorance. There are people in denial over the lasting effect of the inhuman trade in human beings, which has created as well as fed racism for the 10 jubilee years. If this the 2000th year of Christian Era is to mark a significant departure from this unjust relationship then we who call ourselves Christians must be on the march for debt release and economic empowerment of the Third World which includes us Africans.

Our vision-impaired existence makes us prone to carry on as if nothing is happening around us that needs God's vengeance. Ignorance of what environmental degradation means to our planet and our lives; Ignorance of the real proportions of the HIV/AIDS pandemic; even ignorance as to why we are poor and sick; ignorance of our captivity to values that are contrary to Gospel demands, need to disappear.

In contemporary Ghana our bondage is expressed as bondage to Satan and evil spirits and unhelpful ancestral spirits. I would like to suggest that while we deliver ourselves from these negative influences we should think of how to free ourselves from self-seeking greed and wanton wastefulness of earth's scarce provisions for our lives and sheer careless living. Jubilee is stocktaking and starting afresh and all of us have to be involved in this exercise.

Recently the Institute of African Women in Religion and Culture of Trinity Theological Seminary and The Circle of Concerned African Women - Theologians held a conference at the nurses Hostel on October 6-8, 1999 with the theme "the Concept of Jubilee from African Women's Perspectives". These were women ready to speak because silence is no longer an option and we had a lot to say and to pray. We were asking ourselves supposing the G8 really cancelled Africa's debts, what would we do with the breathing space. What are our priorities? We have to plan this as we pray in anticipation of the Jubilee becoming a reality. We asked ourselves about communal priorities and social justice. We asked is there anything we ourselves should be doing in this year of jubilee?

We have to confess our collective sins, so we can have the demons of low self-esteem as Black people exorcised. Our governments seem impotent in the face of the market economy. Our keynote address at the conference was given by a Zambian woman, Omega Bula, but all of us present including the Ghanaians felt she was talking about our own countries. Her focus was on globalization, defined as the "integration of world markets no matter the level of development of the particular economy" Globalization has resulted in a few people that hold and manage power. She led us to discover the essence of jubilee as establishing social equality, restoring the rights of the poor, respecting the dignity of all and honoring the identity of the other.

Jubilee and us

The year 2000 marks a jubilee that brings us the opportunity to atone for slavery, colonial exploitation, ecological injustice and mal-administration of national affairs. The year of jubilee will impact our lives as we wake up to the needs around us, and work on them both in our Church and our workplace, in our homes, and among ourselves as women dealing justly with the weak and nurturing the dignity of the other, will be an act of jubilee. So sound the trumpet, proclaim release to the captives. In Leviticus 25:8-14 we are called to proclaim freedom **to all the inhabitants of the land**. People chained to their wealth, afraid to fall on bad days cannot live by faith and by hope, chained to profit they dare not see the human face of the negative aspects of globalization.

Proclaim release to those who cannot pass through the dense smoke of poverty to see the God of life.Proclaim release to victims of Trokosi and of ritual murders Proclaim release to victims of HIV/AIDS and the violations of our humanity. Proclaim release to those whom so called disabilities have marginalized because we have not learnt to harness their abilities.

Sound the trumpet; proclaim release to all thrown into our streets by mis-education and lack of direction. Proclaim release to all who fear being plagued by demons and witches. Preach from all pulpits and platforms, at synods and at gatherings, from all available media that the ban on the leadership of women has been lifted.

"Sound the trumpet" should be accompanied by serious legwork and all hands on deck. It should involve our whole being and the whole people. If the wall of Poverty, ignorance, exploitation, and injustice are to crumble and fall like the walls of Jericho and the Berlin wall that mocked the brokenness of our world,

we should all bring out the *mmenson* and through them sound the note that the earth belongs to God and we are only tenants here for a little while.

What do we want to leave posterity? If we can face this question, I know the year of jubilee will have an impact on our day-to-day living.

Proclaim Release to African Women

- African women read Ephesians 1:3 and claim the gifts of the jubilee
- The author teaches the restoration of blessings in Christ. African Women hear this as the sound of the trumpet that calls Huu---u
- African woman is lifted from the degradation of sin
- African woman is lifted from worthlessness
- African woman is lifted from inferiority
- African woman is lifted from beneath the hells of domination

- Christ has removed the alienation from God
- The blessings of God give her the crown of honor again
- She once more shares dominion (authority) as in Gen. 1:28
- She once more shares fruitfulness
- The fruits of the spirit are hers also as the chains fall off her potential to be in ministry
- So to-day the call from Africa reaches your ears
- Huu --- are you with us
- Are you with us as we march towards full humanity?

(This paper is a modified version of the report of the conference given to the Tri-ennial Assembly of women of Presbyterian Church USA in 2000).

What does the concept of Jubilee mean to us as African Women : given our current economic, social, political, cultural and religious situations?

Araba Ata Sam

Reading the book of the prophet Isaiah Chapter 61 today, it seems as if the chapter was written for this age. Verses 1 and 2 (which are quoted in St. Luke 4 v. 18-19) say:

"The Spirit of the Sovereign Lord is on me,
because the Lord has anointed me
to preach good news to the poor.
He has sent me to bind up the broken-hearted,
to proclaim freedom for the captives
and release from darkness the prisoners;
to proclaim the day of vengeance of our God"
St. Luke says: " —— and recovery of sight to the blind,
to release the oppressed,
to proclaim the year of the Lord's favour"

These are promises that in our situation today seem impossible to be fulfilled. The concept of Jubilee refers to a situation where the people were set free from their bondage every fifty years. It was very good news to them!

In our current situation as African women, the promises seem very far off. The good news has been preached to the poor, of whom the women form the majority; but the good news promises **abundant life** which has eluded most women.

Poverty seems to have a feminine face; and this has been the result of wars, ethnic conflicts, international debts, etc. which always leave women the poorer. Many women today have no social life to talk of because their economic situation gives them no social status.

" The spirit of the Lord——— to bring recovery of sight to the blind". Many of our women are vsion impaired with regard to what is happening around them. There is so much ignorance that they do not see why there is so much fuss about the disease, filth and poverty which are engulfing them. They have not "recovered their sight" to enable them improve the situation in which they find themselves.

.... to bind up the brokenhearted".

Many women are broken-hearted because of unjust laws. They are raped, and see their daughters raped, but the perpetrators are not given just punishment. They suffer all forms of abuse and violence in the home, work-places and in the community, yet they see no end to it. In many cultures, women continue to suffer widowhood rites - a dehumanizing condition which leaves them devastated. In some cases, they lose their property and have to depend on relatives.

.... "to release the oppressed". Women are oppressed by the economic, social, political and cultural situations. Government policies of retrenchment, freezing of wage/salary increases etc., that have created hardships affect women more, because they have to run the household. Salaries of husbands and children have remained static for years, and yet prices keep shooting up. Countries are riddled with huge debts which can never be repaid

Cultural taboos restrict and oppress some women. There are yet other women who feel that religious norms prevent them from leading the sort of life they prefer to lead eg. freedom to be a second wife in a Christian religion.

"Proclaiming the year of the Lord's favour" - the year of Jubilee in which we should celebrate; but can we celebrate when there is no sign of jubilee? Can we celebrate when there is so much rape, abuse and violence? Wars in Sierra Leone, Angola, Congo, Eritrea etc. have left in their wake countless problems for women many of whom have been widowed, have become pregnant from rape, or have become refugees.

God promised to "bestow a crown of beauty", but Africa is covered with a crown of ashes; God promised "the oil of gladness", instead there is mourning everywhere. God also promised a "garment of praise", but there is the spirit of despair everywhere. We know from God's promises that He loves justice and hates robbery and iniquity. Because we believe in His promises, we will not allow the spirit of despair to overshadow us. For we know that at the appropriate time, we will "receive a double Portion instead of disgrace rejoice in our inheritance and have everlasting joy".

We only have to believe in His infinite love, trust Him completely by casting our burden on Him and obeying His commands. So let us together join in this Jubilee prayer.

THE JUBILEE PRAYER

Our sovereign Lord and Creator!
We pray to you this year of Jubilee
and claim the fulfillment of your promises,
for you have never failed us'
Everlasting God, Creator of the universe,
the good news of abundant life on earth
has been overshadowed by our wickedness,
injustice and greed, resulting in poverty!

Great Physician and compassionate God,
You promised recovery of sight to the blind.
But we are blinded by ignorance and disease;
and we are engulfed by filth and greed.

Our Saviour and gracious Lord,
You promised us release from bondage.
But our lives are entangled by debts ' taboos,
tribal norms and unrealistic priorities.

In this year of Jubilee, merciful Lord,
Grant us the courage and fortitude
To withstand oppression and social vices
which have become obstacles to your promises;

So that we will be free,
Free from debts and violence!
May your will be done on earth.
Amen.

Araba Ata Sam

A message from women of the Jubilee conference

October 5th – 10th 1999

The Institute facilitated the Ghana Chapter of the Circle of Concerned women Theologians' celebration of the 10th Anniversary of the Convocation of African Women Theologians in Ghana. (It was at this convocation that the Circle of Concerned African Women Theologians was inaugurated). This Jubilee conference is the first of biennial Pan-African conferences that the Institute plans to offer as a continuing forum for examining issues of women, culture and religion.

October 1989 saw the ***"out-dooring"*** ceremony for African women in theology. It was to tell Ghana, Africa and the whole world that African women do indeed study religion, research religious issues and do write books on religion. Above all it was to tell all and sundry that women do want to see religion playing a life-giving and life-enhancing role in the lives of all Africans.

At the conference were twelve international participants who made their contribution to the discussion on the theme **Jubilee 2000: Women's Visions.** The Keynote address, given by Ms Omega Bula of Zambia, posed the critical question,

> ***"When the Jubilee 2000 movement would have succeeded in obtaining the cancellation of the financial debts of the world's poorest*** **nations,** ***how will the new 'lease of life' affect African women and the families they care for?"***

Responses to the Jubilee challenge came from the depth of the hearts of ten women: three Ghanaians, three Nigerians, one Kenyan, two South Africans and one from Lesotho.

The stories of women's experiences told by these women are horrific. What we have seen here in Ghana of murders of women, reinforce the horror of women's lives all over Africa. Moreover they show up our African communities as less than life-giving. The women lament as their cries beat against the heart of God. Do people in power in Africa hear their dirge?

From these **stories** and the many plenary interventions, workshops and discussions, we share with you the challenges posed by the Circle of Concerned African Women Theologians:

- After the Cancellation of Debts; What then?
- Will our communities be any more gender-sensitive?
- Will justice for women become a way of life in Africa?
- Women work and pray for life for all; will African leaders accompany women's efforts with life giving actions?
- Can we hold governments and religious bodies accountable for the well-being of women?

To concretize the concerns of the Circle in Ghana, the conference began the process of raising one billion cedis for the building of Talitha Qumi Centre to house the Institute of African Women in Religion and Culture, which Trinity Theological College (now seminary) inaugurated in March 1999. The building will be in memory of all MOTHERS; our Mothers of Africa and all the world - past and present, women whose contributions to Africa have not been acknowledged.

Looking at what is happening to women in Ghana, we could not jubilate. We could only mourn and wail. How can we jubilate when so many women are being brutally murdered? How can we jubilate when every time we turn the pages of a national newspaper we find a woman violated? How can we jubilate when our TVs reveal the violence done to women? How can we jubilate when the radio bursts our ear with the suffering of women? How can we jubilate when we do not ban men's songs that say "women, what ever you do, you are under us?"

When women suffer, men suffer. When women suffer children suffer. When women suffer, the nation suffers. We therefore will call the whole nation to a national day of mourning for the murders of women and the rape of babies.

It is a curse on this nation if grief remains unexpressed. It is a curse when the murderers are not apprehended. It is a curse when we seem callous and unconcerned.

We are therefore, soliciting your good will to call on all Ghanaians to be vigilant so that these atrocities are completely wiped out from this beautiful nation of ours.

Report of the Conference

Jubilee 2000 became meaningful through this Conference. African Women theologians became a part of the worldwide movement for the cancellation of the financial debts of the world's economically disadvantaged nations. A keen cord was struck among African women and their guests, who met at the celebrations in October 1999. As women who, since 1989, organized themselves into a Circle of Concerned African Women Theologians, the concept of jubilee became particularly relevant because the centre of the Circle has always been faith.

Viewing jubilee from the perspective of religion we affirmed the principle as embodied in the five pillars of Islam, the Judeo-Christian principle of release for the captives and we honoured the African practice of hospitality and making space for the new comer.

That was what brought us together for four days of deliberations, which led to strategies and resolutions for action. We believed in and worked through an analysis of situations in seeking realistic processes that would yield results. As religious women, we believed that peoples and institutions can change and so we decided to remain in prayer that Africa does indeed step into a new Millennium.

Debt Free

After a brilliant keynote by Omega Bula in which she thoroughly analyzed the economic implications of the debt burden on Africa and Africans, the ensuing workshops and plenaries left no doubt as to the realities of what needed to be done. We agreed with her to join in announcing to all that Jubilee is about establishing social equality, restoring the rights of the poor, respecting the dignity of all and honoring the identity of the others. No doubt the time had come to open our mouths because silence was no longer a viable option. All aspects of life in Ghana and all other countries represented were going to honor God's declaration of jubilee to all.

Other papers were delivered and there were theological reflections on various aspects of life.

Other activities included a celebration honoring the Initiator of the Circle, our sister, Mercy Amba Oduyoye for the dedicated trailblazing for women in Theology over the years that led to the Circle and the Institute. The beauty of this celebration is that it came as a surprise to her coupled with a well deserved recognition of her 87 year old mother who was present. The spontaneity and enthusiasm with which the assembly joined in this event justified our decision to honor those who deserve honor while they can enjoy it. (See pictures) Books of the Circle were on display and a booklet of poems by Mercy Oduyoye produced by the Institute was introduced.

One of the highlights of the celebration was the launching of the fund-raising for the building of the Talitha Qumi Centre. This would be the fulfillment of the Circle's dream of a place by women for women, where theology, religion and culture will meet and merge in that well tried experiment to bring understanding of the affairs of God. The Circle seeks a safe space to experience a clear vision of God's project for humankind, now complicated by human misunderstanding. Amidst drumming and dancing the first million of a billion-cedi fund was raised.

The participation was most encouraging and consisted of members of the clerical and lay ministries, church Women's Groups, Women's organizations, Muslim women's Groups, students from high schools (both boys and girls), universities and theological institution's faculty especially from Trinity Theological Seminary, dance and choral groups. In all about 400persons participated in the plenaries and 120 in the workshops and 40 in the seminars.

Thus over the four days we experienced Jubilee in celebration, a Ghanaian response, an international participants' response and in between, serious reflections on the issues raised in the presentations. The variety issues, uniformity with which each country described the plight of women in today's world, made the closing ceremonies one of ceremonial weeping for the violence and destruction. Evidence was then current in Ghana with the up to then twenty-one murders of women in an area of Accra where the perpetrators were never found. During the ceremonial ritual of pouring water to symbolize the tears of women world wide the heavens joined in sympathy as the rains came down in solemn agreement. Yes indeed all agreed that women's tears should be shed on each others behalf and these would reach and touch the heart of the Almighty. The Institute is calling prayer retreats on Violence against women, while the Circle continues the research into the religion and culture that under girds all this.

PART III

METHODOLOGY

Letter of Invitation to Special Guests

WAY FORWARD - GREATER ACCRA

MARCH 16 - 19 - 2000

It is almost a year now that Trinity Theological Seminary inaugurated the Institute of African Women in Religion and Culture. One of the programmes of the institute is to hold Way Forward Seminars around the country to promote gender sensitivity in religious and theological institutions.

Since then we have had Way Forward Peki, Ho, Cape Coast and Kumasi. It is now the turn of Greater Accra. **You are invited to the opening event, which will be held on the 17th March from 09.00 - 13.00 at Trinity Theological Seminary. The theme is "Overcoming Violence: A challenge to Ghana's faith communities".**

We are writing to request your presence at this important event, as we are aware of your commitment to addressing the issues of violence in our community. Your presence will serve as a strong support the resolution of violence in Ghana.

We thank you for your participation in this important event.

Sincerely yours

MERCY AMBA ODUYOYE
DIRECTOR

Invitation to Youth Forum Held in Winneba.

October 2000 Conference- "New Beginning Religious Resources for Creating Gender Sensitivity in Our Nation"

To Principals of selected Senior Secondary Schools in Winneba, Apam and Swedru:

Given the need for religion to contribute positively to the lives of women, Trinity Theological Seminary has established a project on African Women in Religion and Culture. To introduce the project, as well as get the input of People of Faith, series of seminars are being held around the country. They have been named 'Way Forward Seminars' to indicate the objective of seeking a fresh approach to issues of the relations of women and men in Religion and Society, and to foster gender sensitivity and justice for women and children.

In the past year these seminars have been held in Peki, ho, Cape Coast, Kumasi, Bolga, Greater Accra and Abetifi. Before we proceed any further it behoves us to evaluate these efforts in order to chart a course that will make the project more effective. It is in pursuance of this that we are calling a national conference in October.

The Conference is scheduled from October 4th to 8th 2000. The venue is the National Sports College, Winneba, and this note is to invite your participation and to invite your school to send a delegation of thirty students (girls and boys) to participate in the conference on Saturday October 7th, 2000 from 8.30 to 12noon, designated "Youth Forum on Gender". We would like also to float the theme of the Conference as an Essay Competition to be judged at the school at your convenience but before the Conference dates. The first three winners will receive prizes. Again we would like your suggestions. We are able to budget a sum of a hundred thousand cedis for the essay competition-

The best essays will be read by their authors at the Youth Forum on Saturday. The conference organizers are able to contribute the fuel for the trip and to provide the students with snacks at noon. By this we also invite the staff of the school for the session.

Thank you very much for your kind consideration of this request.

God bless you all.

Mercy Amba Oduyoye.
Director

FLOATING THE JUBILEE CONFERENCE IN GHANA (A BROCHURE)

THE THEME OF THE CONFERENCE

"The concept of Jubilee from African Women's perspective"

THE VENUE: Nurses' Hostel behind SECAPS HOTEL Tetteh Quarshie Circle, Accra.

Background:

This is a celebration to mark the Tenth anniversary of the Convocation of The Circle of Concerned African Women Theologians. We are not yet 50years old but we feel the Jubilee, we feel the liberation God has granted us by opening our lips when silence was no longer a viable option.

In October therefore we shall not only celebrate our existence but also honor God's declaration of Jubilee in all aspect of our life together in Ghana.

- Papers will be delivered on the theology of Jubilee
- Theological Reflections on various aspects of Life
- Bible study workshops to contextualize the Jubilee
- Jubilee 2000 and Debt release
- Sharing our thoughts through publications (Launching of Books by Circle Women)
- Fund raising

SESSIONS

6TH OCTOBER

OPENING

Open to general Public, Church Women's Groups, Women's Organizations, Muslim Women's Organizations, Muslim Women's Groups e.t.c at the Nurses Hostel.

7th OCTOBER

Panel discussions of Workshop

THEME: *"African Women's Perceptions of the Concept of Jubilee"*

8th OCTOBER

*Continuation of discussion

*Closing Session

Fees

A token fee of ¢ 5,000 per participant towards feeding cost.

Participation

All the Ghanaian Circle members and the invited guests.

Editors Note:

A separate personalized invitations went to members of the Circle who belong to the Study Commission on Multi-Cultural and Multi-Religious Living.

PROGRAMME PLANNING

Planning Way Forward in Obo

From: Roelof & Jacolien Wolters <rtc@libr.ug.edu.gh>
To: Prof. M.A. Oduyoye <talitha@ghana.com>
Subject: Way Forward in Obo
Date: Saturday, June 10, 2000 5:00 PM Dear Ladies,

We are trying to have the Way Forward Seminar for SSS youth in Obo 15 July 2000. Next Monday some of us are going there to see how and what we will do. We want to inform you about this date and ask if it is convenient for you. If not, please send us the dates that are possible for you. We thought that the programme could be the same as in Abetifi: in the morning a presentation and time for questions and remarks after this workshop. It would be nice if we could do a kind of gender-sensitivity test, either before the meeting or as a workshop. Because you told us about a course on this subject, do you know if they have something like that?

We planned an evaluation meeting on 8 July with the representatives of the women groups from the April meeting, to hear what they have done with their plans in their places.

We look forward to hearing from you soon.

Letter to Co-ordinators of Previous Seminars

October National conference 2000

Dear Friends,

We just completed the survey for the logistic needs of the above programme. The conference will be held at the National Sports College, Winneba. The dates are: October 4-8, 2000. The theme of the conference is "New Beginnings: Religious Resources for Creating Gender Sensitivity in our Nation".

We invite your participation in the following way:

i. Attend the conference for the full period and report on the event you organized.

ii. Invite 5 other persons to come with you, preferably those who helped you to plan or were resource persons in the event you held.

iii. Hold brainstorming session where you are to gather ideas on how the project may be made more effective so that you and one of the persons with you could report at the conference.

Tentatively the programme is as follow:

General Structure of the October Conference 2000

October 4th Wednesday	-	All arrive
October 5th Thursday	-	Participants workshop
October 6th Friday	-	am. Public Opening
		pm. Participants workshop
October 7th Saturday	-	am. Youth Forum
		pm. Participants workshop
October 8th Sunday	-	am. Free/worship
	-	pm. Participants workshop
October 9th Monday	-	Departure

The organizers of the conference are: Dr. Elizabeth Amoah & Ms.Rebecca Dodge

Do stay in touch with them.

Blessings,

Mercy.

Sample Programmes
Inaugural Event

March 13th 99

10.00am - 12noon

1. Opening Prayers - Pamela M. Martin (Women's Hall President)

   Introduction of Chairperson - Rev. Dr A. A. Akrong (Moderator of Institute's Advisory Board)

3. Presentation of programme - (chairpersons) Prof. Marian Addy, (University of Ghana) Legon.

4. Welcome Address - Revd. Dr Dan Antwi, (Principal Trinity Theological College)

5. The Story of the Institute - Mercy Amba Oduyoye, (Director of the Institute)

6. Musical interlude - Police Church Gospel Band

7. Key note address - Prof..Florence Dolphyne (University of Ghana)

8. Panel Presentation on Women in Religion and Culture

   - Christian perspective: Rev. Dr. Emmanuel Martey
   - Muslim perspective: Hajiah Katumi Mahama
   - Cultural perspective: Dr. Elizabeth Amoah

9. Plenary Responses: Open to all.

10. Musical interlude - Police Church Gospel Band.

11. Chairperson's Remarks – Prof..Marian Addy.

12. Induction of Members of the Advisory Board. - Prof. K. A. Dickson.

13. Vote of thanks - Rev. Dr A. A. Akrong.

14. Closing Prayers - Rev. Dinah Abbey Mensah (Member of Advisory Board)

15. Refreshments.

WAY FORWARD SEMINAR- GREATER ACCRA

MARCH 16th – 19th 2000

THEME: *"OVERCOMING* VIOLENCE*: A CHALLENGE TO GHANA'S FAITH COMMUNITIES".*

PROGRAMME OF OFFICIAL OPENING

FRIDAY 7th MARCH, 2000

8.30 - 9.00	Cultural Opening	Dr. Newman's Group
9.00 - 9.30	Seating of people	Chairperson- Dr. Akrong
9.30- 9.45	Opening Prayers	Christian Council
9.40-10. 00	Introductions Musical interlude	Dr. Amoah Women's Fellowship
10.00 -10.45	Theme Address	Dr. Rabiatu Ammah and Dr. Mercy Amba Oduyoye Musical interlude. Kafui's Choir, Achimota School
11.00 - 11.30	Drama on Theme	Lutheran Church Youth
11.30 - 12.00	Name Your Mother' (Fund Raising)	Rev. Laurene Nyarko
12.00 -12.10	Chairperson's Remarks	
12.15 -12.36	Musical Interlude	Dr. Newman's Group
12.30 -13.00	Refreshment	
13. 00 -13.30	**Closing**	
13.30	Seminar Participants depart for Abokobi.	

WAY FORWARD - GREATER ACCRA

THEME - OVERCOMING VIOLENCE: A CHALLENGE TO GHANA'S FAITH COMMUNITIES

SCHEDULE OF ACTIVITES:

Thursday, March 16th, 2000:

Residential participants arrive at Abokobi Presbyterian Women's Training Centre.

Friday, March 17''', 2000:

9: 00am - 1: 00pm	Opening Event: Trinity United Church Trinity Theological Seminary Legon
1: 00pm - 2: 00pm	Residential participants move to Abokobi
2:00pm - 3:30pm	Plenary sessions.
	Open forum on issues raised at official opening
3:30pm -4:30pm	Sub-theme 1 "Single Women and the Church's Responsibility" Rev. C. K. Konadu
4:30pm - 4:45pm	Short break
4:45pm - 5:45pm	Participants special concerns about the theme
6:00pm - 7:00pm	Supper
7:30pm - 8:30pm	Workshop groups

Saturday, March 18th 2000 Workshop Continues

9: 00ain - 10: 00am	"HIV/AIDS: A Death Sentence to Married Women

10: 00am - 11: 00am	Panel on Aspects of Violence Against Women: "Violence Against Women: A Challenge to Christian Theology": Rev. Dr. E. Martey; "Trokosi, a Violation of Human Rights": Rev Walter Pimpong
1 1:00am - 11: 15am	Short Break
11: 15am - 12:15pm	Sub-theme V: "For Theirs is the Kingdom" Rev. Mensah
12:15pm - 2: 00pm	Break
2: 00pm - 3: 00pm	"Rape/Defilement - A Challenge to the Whole Community" Henrietta Mensa-Bonsu, Rev. James Saah
3:00pm - 4:00pm	"The Child Factor in Marriage and the Church's Responsibility Rev. Dr. Emmanuel Asante.
3:30pm - 5:00pm	Workshop Groups
5: 00pm - 6: 00pm	Reports from Groups and Evaluations – Message Reports from Message Committee Evaluation
6:00pm - 7:00pm -	Supper/Closing
Sunday, March 19"', 2000	Breakfast and departure

AFRICAN WOMEN THEOLOGIANS AND JUBILEE 2000

5th to 10th October 1999

Programme

Tuesday 5th October:

Arrival and Registration

Wednesday 6th October:

Celebration of the Convocation of African Women Theologians in 1989

08:00 - 09:30		Registration continues
09:30 - 10:00		Refreshments
10:00 - 10:30		Opening Prayer by Rev Laurene Nyarko Welcome and Introduction of Chairperson by Dr Mercy Amba Oduyoye.
10:30 - 11:00		**Keynote on Jubilee 2000 by Ms. Omega Bula –AACC Canada**
11:00 - 11:30		Discussion/ Ebibindwom Group
11:30 - 12:30		**The Celebration:**
		1989: The Convocation of African Women Theologians in The Story by Dr. Mercy Amba Oduyoye. -Launching of Building Fund for Talitha 'Qumi' Centre Rev. Laurence Nyarko
12:30- 03:00	-	Lunch Break
03:00- 04:00	-	Plenary
		Issues for workshops
04:00-04:30	-	Refreshments
04:30-06:00	-	Workshops

THURSDAY 7th October - The Ghanaian Response

08:30-09:00	-	Meditation
09:00-10:30	-	Plenary Panel on Ghanaian Response to the Jubilee
10:30-11:00	-	Break
11:30-12:30	-	Discussion
12:30-3:00	-	Lunch break
03:00-04:00	-	Plenary
	-	Issues for workshops
04:00-04:30	-	Refreshments
04:30-06:00	-	Workshops

FRIDAY 8th October - Theological Responses to the Jubilee

08:30-09:00	-	Meditation
09:00- !0:30	-	Plenary International Participants
10:30-11:00	-	Break
11:30-12:30	-	Discussion
12 : 30	-	Lunch

AFTERNOON – FREE

SAT **9th October**		Closing Acts
08:30-09:00	-	Meditation
09:00-10:30	-	Plenary: Reports
10:30-11:00	-	Break
11:30-12:30	-	Plenary Discussion and Evaluation
12:30-3:00	-	Lunch break
3:00		Closing Ceremony

COME LET US CELEBRATE

Closing Acts

Singing	-	Madina Group
Opening Prayer	-	Hajia Katumi Mahama
Introduction and Seating of President	-	Mrs. Araba Sam

President's Welcome and Response	-	Rev. Mrs Laurene Nyarko
Introduction of Keynote Speaker	-	Rev. Mrs. Laurene Nyarko
Reflection	-	An International Participant
Singing	-	Madina Group
Symbolic	-	Women's Tears
Prayer in Different Languages		
Celebration in Dance to be led by	-	Ho Circle
		a Participant
Benediction	-	a Pastor.

Editorial Note

Celebrations such as the above and Prayer retreats on Current Concerns like serial murders of women in Ghana are given very minimal structures. Most of the event become 'happenings' with a lot of spontaneous outpourings. They provide a safe-space for the sharing of emotions and our solidarity in Hope.

7

PARTICIPANT INPUT

Group Work
From
A SEMINAR ON OVERCOMING VIOLENCE

MEMBERS:

Mrs. Eva A. Mensah	
Mrs. Harriet Gyampo-Kumi	Secretary
Nana Kate V.T. Abban	Chairman
Pastor Comfort Manda Djamle	
Ms. Edith Awuye	
Mrs. Florence A. Awuku	
Rev. Anthony K. Mensah	A Resource Person
Mrs. Patience Efua Dickson	

This group discussed all the issues, which were presented in the Seminar. In the four workshops spaces provided and continued informally in order to provide this report.

SINGLE WOMEN

- They are described as women who are not with husbands.
- Those who have never married.
- Those who are widowed.
- Those who have married before but are separated or divorced.
- These single women should be given responsibility in the Church. This could be done when their talents have been identified.
- The church should have a holistic programme to cater for the welfare of these people especially the widows. This will help them to cater for themselves and the children left with them. What is normally done in the churches is that they sympathize with them for a short period and they forget about the plight of the widow.

- Churches that have no programmes for the single women should identify and consult other churches who have started long ago.

HIV/AIDS

- The churches should have extensive education for all members of the church. This should include adults/youth/children.

- It has been alleged that some of these young girls who contract the AIDS disease through sex are sex workers. If this is so then, the church should have income generating activities and have micro credit scheme to remove them from that dangerous job.

- Churches should have their own counselling and case units. This will help victims to know that they are still loved.

- Members in the churches should come together and pray for prevention against these diseases.

VIOLENCE AGAINST WOMEN AND THE TROKOSI

It was found that very few educated women suffer domestic violence (physical). Those who do not have the benefit of literacy are more often the victims of this form of violence. If this is so then women should be well educated to know their rights, as education is a tool of empowerment.

The women should be empowered to know their rights and be encouraged to speak out.

Churches should have shelters and refuge homes with well trained counselors to cater for them.

This is because sometimes some of these women are thrown out of their marital homes, and need a safe space or half-way house before they can re-locate.

Education on this issue should be given to all and sundry in the church - the youth/adult and children. This is because even children and babies suffer domestic violence directly or are traumatized by the violence they witness at home.

The church is guilty and must think of ridding itself of the guilt. The church is guilty because some ministers and elders of the church are involved in this abuse of women. The very things they preach are against what they themselves practise.

Editorial Note

On domestic violence of all forms including verbal abuse, bolstering formal research has shown that the educational status of the couple is not a factor. Women of all levels of education including those with doctorates have reported battering.

TROKOSI

- The churches must encourage -and collaborate with the NGO's and organizations dealing with the Trokosi system. They need our encouragement through our prayer and concern.

- The church must speak out for the discontinuance of the system and supporting the law passed on the abolishing of the Trokosi system.

THE CHURCH AND THE CHILDREN

- The church must budget for and take interest in the education and welfare of the children in the church.
- This is because children contribute towards funding the church and even pay tithes and pledges in the churches. Their share must be given back to them through education and their welfare.
- The church should intensify the teaching of the fear of God in children.
- The Christians and other religious groups should teach their members not to leave the upbringing of children to biological families only.
- Parents must be responsible for the holistic training of the children.
- The church must identify and assist the poor members through giving and teaching them some income generating activities.
- Parents must be responsible for training their children to become good citizens.
- The youth and the children should be educated in parenting before they become real mothers and fathers. This will minimise teenage pregnancy and lead the youth to abstain from sex before marriage.

In conclusion churches are advised to stop classism in the church. The church is not a worldly society. The class society discriminate against other members who do not belong to their groups.

AIDS/HIV

1. The main objective should be to:

   - Overcome the AIDS/HIV pandemic
   - Educate the groups we belong to, to understand the scriptural teachings on morality.
   - Churches must be willing to give moral support to the victims and to develop a new image of those living with HIV/AIDS.
   - We need the courage to meet men's groups to present them with our concerns on this scourge.
   - We need to get involved with the programmes of the youth and Sunday school, women groups and others.
   - We need to devise creative ways of presenting this issue for discussion e.g. in drama, poetry reading sessions.

From National Conference 2000

GROUP DISCUSSION
ISSUES TO BE DISCUSSED IN GROUP 1

1. How do we deal with pre-marital sex?

2. What are the various forms of violence and how do we deal with them?

3. How do we use the scripture and traditional beliefs and practices as sources of liberation and not oppression of women?

4. How do we deal with marital problems that lead to divorce?

5. How do we contribute to the liberation and rehabilitation of Trokosi victims ?

6. How do we empower through education and social-cultural development the well-being of the young girls?

DISCUSSIONS

I How do we deal with pre-marital sex?

What is pre-marital sex?

It is having sex before marrying.

It is also having sex before the age of 18 (that is the accepted minimum age of marrying).

SOME CAUSES OF PRE-MARITAL SEX

Lack of Parental Care:

If parents renege their responsibilities as parents, that is providing food, shelter, clothing and other necessities to their wards they tend to go about seeking for where to get these needs. They come across 'benefactors' whose promise of help come with conditions. They finally end up having sex with these poor minors before helping them. These helpers are normally termed as "sugar Daddies and sugar Mummies." This brings us down to the next topic (cause) to be discussed.

Lack of Parental Control: This is when parents allow their children to decide for themselves or make choices on their own. For instance the youth goes out to cinemas, discotheques and the like, and comes in any time they choose. Parents realize that this is actually going on but keep mute. The child becomes part of the peer group he/she wishes.

The Peer Group: This factor is by far the most effective way most youths are being influenced into bad or deviant attitudes. Broken... Homes/ Dissolved marriages: the youth in this situation gives excuses of visiting my mother or father whereas the destination is another place to see his/her partner.

Lack of Education and Counseling: Most people lack proper education on waiting to get married before sex. Hence they indulge themselves before marriage.

The media is also a contributing factor. That T.V. Radio, Audio cassette players, Tape, and videos, the news papers, magazines and bill boards, tend to send wrong messages to young people.

To deal with these problems, discipline must first begin from the various homes. Parents must give their children guidance for a critical approach to the media and in all their relationships with others. Most important is the stress on the old saying "The fear of God is the beginning of wisdom".

What are the various forms of violence, and how do we deal with them? What is violence? As defined in the Ghanaian society violence is:

- A forceful way of getting something from someone.
- Making someone do what he/she dislikes.
- Cruelty or wickedness.
- Impediments in one's way.

Forms of Violence

Domestic violence: Children abuse, parents preventing children from attaining laudable goals, maltreatment of domestic workers, mothers using pepper as suppositories as way of punishing children and the like.

Economic Violence: Gender imbalances in terms of work. Women are denied responsible positions at work places as due them. Only few women are nominated at parliamentary elections.

In education females are sometimes in various homes prevented from attending school. Meanwhile the chance is given to males to have formal education.

Rape is also a form of violence.

EDITORIAL NOTE – Spousal abuse in the form of wife-battering and verbal violence do not feature in this group's report.

REMEDIES

Parents must be educated on how to keep the family. Each must know his/her responsibilities. The idea of gender imbalance must be discarded. Those found as law violators such as rapists, child molesters and robbers must be brought to book.

How do we use the scripture and the Traditional beliefs and practices as sources of liberation and not oppression of women?

When we look into the scripture (Bible), we find men who married more than one wife. Examples of these people are Solomon, David, Jacob and others. The household of Abraham, Sarah and Hagar is another case in point. From these passages, people who practise polygamy justify themselves. Many women however see this type of marriage as oppressive for the women involved and therefore see it as violence against them.

Most people misinterpret the Bible passage on the use of head-kerchief or the covering of the hair, as a symbol of the subjection of women to men. It is the same in the Moslem sector. They consider the traditional beliefs and practices such as widowhood rites, Female Genital Mutilation, Puberty rites and the like forms of oppressions of women in all sectors of society.

To bring relief, spiritual leaders must have the scriptures interpreted and taught in a way that will help eliminate practices such as men cheating on women. Some traditional beliefs and practices may need to be repealed.

How do we contribute to the liberation and rehabilitation of Trokosi victims?

- We should seek God's direction on how to liberate them.

- There must be intensive education through the media, house-to-house teachings on counseling, dramatization of the experiences of the Trokosi victims.
- Concerned people must help family members of Trokosi to overcome the fears they entertain as a result of the beliefs associated with the practice.
- The victims too must receive the above re-education. Church rallies should be held in places where the practice is rampant to enable open discussion of the issues involved.
- The government should legislate laws to banish this system.

EDITORS NOTE – Legislation has been passed, the challenge therefore is monitoring implementation and dealing with violators.

How do we empower through education and socio-cultural development, the well-being of the young girls?

* Parents must motivate their young girls to pursue higher education. They must encourage schooling and show its benefits economic, psychological and others.

* We must discourage early marriages.

* Adultery must be discouraged

* Improve communication in the family

* Barrenness and impotency should not become the cause of violence

* The financial viability of families should lie with both parents,

they should openly discuss financial planning.

* Interference of family members in the affairs of young couples should be discontinued.

Suggestions for Peaceful Family life

- There should be mutual understanding, each must consider the other's views
- There must be trust in terms of finance eg. Transparency on the salary each receives
- The man and the woman must share responsibilities for the education of their children.
- They (man and woman) must have daily devotional time together.
- Each must not take marital problems out of the marriage to family members.
- In terms of barrenness or impotency both must have patience and seek God's intervention. There must be love.
- Couples must plan on how to use movies.
- The man must help the woman in house chores.

Suggestion for the Welfare of Girls

- In the early ages of the girl-child, she must not be introduced to trading or money. (Young girls selling ice water).
- The girl must be helped or educated on how to develop her talents. She must be helped to set goals and develop aspirations in life. The society must be involved in the girl's education.
- The government must give free compulsory education to girls.
- In our schools there must be opportunities given to girls for admission to higher institutions of learning.
- Non-formal education, leading to high self-esteem and poise must become intentional.
- Girls must be enabled to acquire skills and vocations.

GROUP 2

Chairwoman: Mme Florence Awuku
Report Secretary: Mrs. Alice Adade

How do we deal with Pre-marital sex?

Premarital sex is defined as having sex with a woman or man you are not married to. Often this sex before marriage is described as fornication in biblical terms. This is commonly considered as being among the youth.

CAUSES

*Greediness for material things making capital of money

*Lust of the flesh. Desire to experiment.

*Anxiety. Anxious to know what sex is like.

*Influence from peer group. Bad friends

*Ignorance of the risks

*Poor parenting too strict or too liberal

*Irresponsible parents

*Influence from some evil spirits

*Media e.g. Video show, reading pornographic books and magazines

*Rape and defilement.

EDITORIAL NOTE - Evil spirits, satan & demons have become the standard excuse for moral weakness and wickedness especially on the part of men.

Dangers

- Veneral diseases i.e. Sexually Transmitted Diseases STD & AIDS
- Unwanted Pregnancy leading to Abortion and its complication, unwanted children being abandoned; may lead to death.
- Prevent girls from getting good husbands.
- Causes infertility in both men and women
- Boys cannot concentrate on their studies or may suffer psychologically in other ways.
- Boys and girls can drop out from school
- Mental disorders are possible for both.

SOLUTIONS

* Education by parents in early age.

* The parents should be role models for the children

* Devotion: Bible study and prayer with children in the home,

Encourage church going.

* Parents be friends with your children (This applies specially to fathers who do not seem to have time for their children)

* Discipline the children

* Don't take young people to family planning sessions, only counsel him or her with prayers.

What are the various forms of violence against women and how to deal with them?

Violence is described as mistreating a person or relating to a woman, against her will and rights. It can be spiritual, domestic, physical or verbal and open disgrace.

Forms of violence

* Beating the woman
* Torture by overburdening the woman with housework
* An alcoholic husband battering wife when drunk could lead her into depression.
* Suppression by bullying husband who prevents you from earning money.
* Financial cheating – takes your earnings
* Denying you sexual intimacy.
* A man leaving the wife for about ten years to go overseas for another woman
* Widowhood rites, too cruel to talk about.
* The trokosi system

How to deal with these:

* Educate men that women are their better halves not their servants
* Educate the woman mentally and socially to create awareness: Mosques, Churches, groups at place of work and homes should all get involved in this re-education.
* The woman should be financially independent.
* The woman should know her rights and limitations. She must be tactful in her relationships.
* Share our good experience with men, and encourage them to do the same in order to promote mutual learning.

How do we use the scripture and traditional beliefs and practices as sources of liberation and not oppression of women?

- Seek empowering interpretations of the Bible eg the rib was taken from the man's side, so it should be side by side Gen: 2.21. In 1st Peter 3: 7-8, God is telling the man to love and live considerately with his wife bestowing honor on the woman as weaker sex, that your prayers may not be hindered. Col 3: 18-19, John 8: 2-1 1. The woman caught in adultery Mat. 27: 50-54. Jesus is against double standards for women & men in the same church.

- In Islam, women are now allowed in the mosque. They are allowed to study the Koran and Hadith as the men.

- Traditional Beliefs: It is traditionally believed that the woman should not request first for sex. It shows you are a spoiled woman. The men should be aware that women can also request.

- The men should understand the need for family planning to help space childbirth.

- The women should get involved in decision-making.

- The girl-child must have equal access to education.

- Some traditional role differentials are no longer necessary. The woman now can weave kente cloth and can still have children.

- Now the men can help with house work, and remain potent.

- If you don't go through the cruel widowhood rites nothing bad will happen to you as a result of this omission. Awareness is being created.

- Laws are being passed to eliminate oppressive traditional practices including those concerning inheritance.

- Through seminars and education the female genital mutilation is being abandoned.

GROUP 3

What is Pre-Marital Sex

Having sex before marriage. This maybe triggered by very seemingly innocent acts as walking hand in hand.

Entering into such a relationship without formal involvement of the parents of both parties is frowned upon as immoral and risky especially for a girl. We should therefore educate our children from the early age at 8 or 10. If we do not educate them at this age they may be influenced by the peer group. It is better if the youth would abstain from sex. If not, then should use condom. Prevention is better than cure. We are to educate young people religiously on pre-marital sex.

What is Domestic Violence?

Maltreatment in Marriage like:

Beatings, starving, Raping, Female Genital Mutilation or female circumcision, or a man sleeping with a girl friend on his matrimonial bed.

How to deal with domestic violence

Women shouldn't provoke their husbands likewise husbands shouldn't provoke their wives. No spouse deserves to be beaten.

Men should abstain from excessive drinking.

Both parties should respect each other.

Matrimonial bed must not be shared by any third party.

How to overcome these Violent Acts

You first inform an elderly or respected person who lives in your neighborhood. When this continues you better inform a leader in church or the Priest to talk to both parties or a relative who support the marriage. Is it advisable to have joint account? This is a frequently asked question because of the risks that a husband. may use this to curb a wife's authority over her own earnings.

How do we use the scripture and Traditional beliefs and Practices as sources of Liberation and not oppression of women?

We are to read our Bibles and pray and fast. There are many passages that give us courage.

For example Exodus 14 verse 14 says be silent, God will fight for you and Psalm 23 says the Lord is my shepherd. It is only God who can solve every problem.

> And in Traditional Society, They give advice to be patient and to have self control. There is a proverb says *Ntoboase wie nkonimdi*, another says *Akyer- akyer w⊃ n'afe.* We shouldn't contact any fetish priest for any help. We should always rely on God. A family which prays together stays together.

How Can We Deal With Marital Problems that Lead to Divorce ?

Contact responsible elderly persons within the neighborhood to bring the relatives of the couple together including the elderly persons for arbitration. Church counsellors and priests too may bring reconciliation. These are groups that can help the couple to find the root cause of the problem. Some of the common causes are adultery, stealing, misunderstanding, financial mismanagement. Others are laziness, unemployment of the man and drunkenness and violence. After the arbitration some couples decide not to reconcile and then divorce ensues.

How do we contribute to the liberation and rehabilitation of trokosi victims?

* The churches should pressurize the government to ensure the elimination of this practice.

* The government, churches and the NGOs should work hard to liberate them.

* People should pray and fast to support the actions.

How do we empower people through education and socio-cultural development?

* Both boys and girls should be treated equally especially in education.

* Equal employment opportunities for people with equivalent skills.

* Equal sharing of house chores by all who inhabit the house.

GROUP FOUR

ISSUES FOR GROUP DISCUSSION.

How do we deal with pre-marital sex? Looking at the causes we have the following

* Lack of self control on the part of both sexes
* Lack of education
* Poverty and Financial problems
* Divorce- Parents becoming unconcerned about their children
* Peer-Group influences
* Lost of pride in virginity

Solutions

* Education - Parents and teachers must take it upon themselves to educate young girls and boys about the dangers of pre-marital sex such as sexually transmitted diseases, pregnancies etc.
* There should be cordial communication between parents and children where both parties can voice out personal problems for solution.
* Parents should not overly restrict children
* The pride of virginity should be restored.
* Parent be concerned about the welfare of their children.

What are the various forms of violence and how do we deal with them?

Forms of violence are as follows:

- Psychological – using one's moral and spiritual authority to intimidate others.
- Physical violence – most commonly, doing damage to a person's body, causing pain and discomfort.
- Economic violence, impoverishing others.
- Social Violence, using class, race, ethnicity and other differences to cause disadvantage to others.
- Cultural Violence, widowhood and other cultural rites that may result in the above forms of violence.
- Sexual violence, harassment, rape, defilement.
- Domestic violence, any of the above that is perpetrated by family members and others who live with them.

Solutions:

* There should be effective communication between couples
* There should be commitment
* Wives should be submissive to their husbands and husbands should love their wives as they love themselves.
* Concerning spiritual violence, women must have a firm foundation in religion to avoid running after 'spiritual giants' for free deliverance.
* Positive traditional values should be restored.

How do we use the scriptures and traditional believes and practices as sources of liberation and not oppression for women?

* There should be a second look at some traditional beliefs such as female genital mutilation. The scriptures too should be interpreted to empower women. An example in the bible is the covering of the hair which some men are using to suppress their wives while the same scripture is used to beautify the hair.

* Women should discuss such traditional practices with husbands and children.

* Women should voice out the dangers of such practices since they are always the victims.

How can we deal with marital problems that lead to divorce?

* There should be understanding, patience, forgiveness and love in marriage.
* Wives should submit to their husbands and husbands should love their wives as scripture demands.
* Wives should co-operate with their in-laws
* There should be communication and cordial relationships between married couples.

How do you contribute to the liberation and rehabilitation of Trokosi victims?

* Religious groups can visit towns where we have these Trokosi shrines and organize programmes. Through that they can present the gospel. They can also make donation in the form of cash or needed items, to support the victims.

* Victims who are back home can be adopted and trained by benevolent societies in bread baking, weaving, leatherwork etc.

How do we empower the girl through education and socio-cultural development?

* Girls should be educated to their fullest potential, to the best of the ability of the parents.

* Girls should take part in political discussions to enhance their understanding of socio cultural issues.

Editorial: As is the practice at weddings, Christians ignore the fact that the household code in Ephesians 5 could begin at verse 21. Not that the Greek original had no sub-headings or verses. In your Bible read verse 21 which says Be subject to one another out of reverence for Christ. (New English/NRSV). Give way to one another in obedience to Christ.(Jerusalem Bible).

... submitting to one another in the fear of God. (NKJV). Submit yourself to one another because of your reverence for Christ. (Good News). "Be committed to one another out of reverence for Christ." The inclusive version should be the watch word for Christian marriage.

ESSAYS OF YOUNG PEOPLE

Topic: CAN RELIGION HELP WOMEN AND MEN LIVE TOGETHER AS PARTNERS?

Emmanuel Eyiah-Donkor
Winneba Secondary School

Religion is a particular system of belief in a supreme Being who made the world and can control it. This supreme Being is 'Onyankopon (Omnipotent) Twerduampon (Rock of Ages) Onyame' (Provider), Who when one has is full with His provisions. Among Ghanaians, almost everybody believes in this Supreme Being whether Traditional, Islamic, or Christian.

A partner is a person who shares or contributes in an activity, be it in games such as tennis, dance, business, leisure or in women and men's relationships.

For the purpose of this essay, women and men living together as partners suggests marriage. Partners are therefore expected to be respected, dignified and honored. There must be trust. Without trust, partnership cannot work because of suspicion. Where there is lack of trust, partnership breaks down. Where cheating is suspected , if it is in business, the business would earn lesser profits. If it is between women and men, it would be landing on rocks. In both cases, the objectives are not achieved. Collapse and divorce may occur.

Living together in the context of this essay means marriage till death. It is a relationship where partners are together, sleeping under one roof most of the time, share the same bed and take decisions with mutuality.

The Akan traditional word for marriage is 'Awar'. Awar is associated with being long.

Marriage is therefore expected to be long lasting -until death separates the partners.

Traditional religion believes in *awar*. However it is polygamous. In such marriages the tendency is for the man to control all the activities in the home. The idea of equal partnership is absent. There is little room for trust. Cheating and oppression are rampant. The women seldom take part in decision making affecting their own well-being. Divorce is very easy under this system because of unequal partnership.

Partnership between women and men (marriage) under the Islamic religion is not too different from traditional religious system. Polygamy is glorified. It has some of the disadvantages of the traditional religion. Women have limited human rights such as the right to work and earn income. Due to suppression in polygamy, the partnership has a weak foundation. Divorce is also very easy.

Christian marriage is monogamous. Women and men in marriage shall be one flesh. Matthew 19: 5-6 instructs that "what God has joined together let no man put asunder." We are also informed that it is out of the man's ribs that Eve was formed (Genesis 2:22).

Thus Christian marriage has symbols showing equal partnership, honor and respect.

God, the Founder of marriage, gave certain essential conditions, these are:

Monogamous marriage, everlasting partnership, divorce only where there is adultery. Adultery is the only condition God allows for a separation. This not withstanding, the adulterer can be forgiven and be reunited to the spouse. This shows that God is totally against divorce. I Peter Chapter 3 verse 1 instructs women to be submissive and to show honor to their husbands. Like wise, the husbands are also to understand their wives, give them love, honor, compassion, respect and show temperance. They are to stay with their wives and have common ownership of the material things of life, which come to them by God's grace (Peter 3:7)

From the above discussion, sustainability in marriage is only possible under God's principles as outlined above especially, the principles of monogamy and equal partnership.

The question then arises: why can't women and men live together as partners? Political, economic, social, cultural and religious circumstances of partnership are the causes of unstable relationships.

In politics, partners may have different views and therefore may belong to different parties. The numerous civil wars, especially in Africa, may separate partners.

Economic empowerment of women has made many women to be financially independent. Some in consequence, have shown disrespectful behavior, Also some men envy their wives. Loss of jobs by either of the spouses may create economic hardship because they can't make ends meet. There is also a general increase in poverty, especially in developing countries, causing frustration in the partnership. Social attitudes have changed. Materialism is on the increase. The pornographic media have helped to increase immorality among partners. All these have shaken foundations of partnership.

Negative imported cultures such as homosexuality have also contributed. Many religious organizations have allowed for easy marriages, multiple marriage, same-sex marriage and easy divorce. Many clergymen have not become role models in the society. News about such pastors and married church leaders committing adultery, divorcing, raping, practising homosexuality and having girl friends are part of the problems which have made concerned citizens to ask whether religion can help women and men live together as partners. (Ref..Daily Graphic Editorial August 22, 2000; Daily Graphic, August 24, 2000 p.7. 'These men of anointing' by E.A. Arthur)

Counselling from parents based on the Bible can help women and men live together as partners. Such parents can encourage the partners to fast and pray faithfully so that God would intervene positively in their relationship.

Moral education in schools must not be treated lightly but as a serious subject which aims at developing morally upright students, who would take women's and men's relationship as partners seriously in future. When this is done news of serial murders, mob-attacks, unruly youths which are threats to a peaceful and stable society would reduce.

Teachers and all those who impart knowledge to the youth also need to be strong in the Christian faith and practices so that they can impact these on the students.

Above all, if the clergymen and senior members of the society would lead exemplary lives as role models to members of their churches and insist that all members adhere to the principles of God in the Bible as discussed above, this question shouldn't arise. I therefore hold the opinion that religion specially the Christian religion can help women and men live together as partners.

CAN RELIGION HELP WOMEN AND MEN LIVE TOGETHER AS PARTNERS

Extract from a Student Essay

Religion is a system of belief and worship which brings people together since they have a common belief. Partners can be defined in this context as people related through marriage or sex.

Religion cannot help women and men live as partners. This is so, because religion can be just a cover-up of an individual's ideology concerning some basic things in life. Individual differences make it difficult for two people to live together peacefully, unless there are the elements of forgiveness, tolerance, selflessness and faithfulness called love. Several marriages have failed because women have been forced on men they do not love. The reason is that since they belong to the same religion, the elders think they can cope well. Therefore the women remain unhappy in the relationship.

REPORT OF A PARTICIPANT IN THE KWAHU SEMINARS

Mary Nsiah (Church of Pentecost, Nkwatia-Kwahu)

To organize the seminar, every local council of churches and women's fellowship was invited to send a representative preferably a woman. This became the planning team that put together the specific concerns of women in the Kwahu area.

The team organized four brain storming sessions one on HIV/AIDS, another on peace, a third one on conflict resolution and a fourth on politics as elections were drawing near.

On April 15th, we had an open day presentation on the subject and then continued in workshops for about three days with three members of each community. In the meeting we found that in Kwahu Areas men don't help the women. Also women are not in leadership positions.

We talked about marriage and how it is guided by culture and religion.

We also talked about tradition and how it influences our lives today.

In the Way Forward Seminar the organizers were Mercy Amba Oduyoye and Mrs. Jacoliin Wolter of Abetifi Ramseyar Center.

Mrs. Mercy Oduyoye gave the address. She was the guest speaker. She talked about culture and Religion in our marriage. She said that in our culture a woman should not beat a man or use her hand to slap a man but a man can slap a woman, use his leg to kick a woman like playing a ball. This she said was not good.

She said the Akan like marriage so they tell the girl "go to kitchen, learn how to cook". But the boy they tell him learn very hard so that you get money. If a boy and a girl are sitting they will call the girl go and do this, clean the bowls, sweep but they are all human beings.

She also said in Akan culture if you cook a fowl there are certain parts which only a man should eat. Often this is the best part so they say. If there is a conflict between a man and a woman they will collect eggs for the **man** but if a man offend the woman they will say forgive him because of the children forgive him. Some men don't look after their children because they say the woman is taking the children to her family.

When people talk about creation we note that God created both man and woman. So man cannot use a woman as he likes.

Man as the head does not mean he has power over his wife or his children. It means he is the one from whom good things are expected.

The head is where the resources of the family come from. The man is the life of the woman. If the man is the head it doesn't mean that he should cheat her.

The blessing in marriage is children but if there are no children only the woman is blamed. If it comes to praying and fasting only the woman is active. Only the woman sweeps, cooks, does the washing, prepares the fire wood and she also trades. The man will not help. When he comes from work or from farm he will go after another woman. The men keep their money secret from the women. Some men give very little chop money but when they go out to the chop bar, they spend about ¢5,000 there, instead of adding it to the chop money he will not do that. To end the speech she told us that if you look in your partner's eye you see yourself in the eye ball. So if you help each other it will bring peace in the marriage or between man and woman.

Thank you.

Issues Raised For Follow Up

*Gender biases occasioned by traditional religious beliefs (focus on trokosi)

*Gender sensitivity in the context of the emerging tourist industry

*Women and Economic Independence

*Gender biases and their effect on women's development

*The Factor of Gender and the Stability of Marriages in Ghana

*Gender, Power and Violence in Ghana

*Street Children and Migrant Self-employed girls and young women

*Education of the girl child

*Single Parenting

*Need to understand the structures of injustice and violence

*The challenge of women as leaders in the church and society

*The need to understand the nature of scripture (Koran and Bible) and Ghanaian ethnic traditions as source of authority

*Religion and HIV/AIDS.

8

APPENDICES

APPENDIX I

Open Prayer at Inaugural Event

Spirituality of Plurality

Pamela Martin

Almighty God and Heavenly father. We thank you for today. We thank you for this gathering which is unto you.

We praise and adore you for who you are, Almighty Creator who made us all in your own image.

We acknowledge your wisdom in Creation that made us all different male and female, Old and young, all races, all Creeds all traditions and Cultures.

We thank you for the wisdom given to those who have brought this idea we celebrate today to fruition.

Be present in our midst, and give us open minds and hearts to understand your will and purpose for this occasion.

We thank you for your mercy that enabled us to travel from near and far to get here. May we not depart from here empty handed.

We bless you for all those who have given of their time, talent, resources and energy to put today's function together. Replenish them a hundred and thousand fold according to your faithfulness

Bless all those who speak or play any part no matter how small, in today's occasion. Let us today be the example of the perfect unity of service expected of all who believe in you and strive to create that World where there are no prejudices, no hatreds, no discrimination but peace and love.

We are all your Children and you love us all. May we together strive to earn your love as we learn to love and understand each other. We stand upon your promise that guarantees that we will receive all we ask from you in faith and thanksgiving in Jesus Name.

AMEN

APPENDIX II

Communique from National Conference

Under the auspices of the Institute of Women in Religion and Culture, a three day seminar was held at Abokobi on the theme "Overcoming Violence: A Challenge to Ghana's Faith Communities".

We, the participants of this seminar, have come together as people of the main religious traditions of Ghana, (Christianity, Islam and indigenous Traditional religion)to discuss responses of our respective faith communities to violence. We reflected on the increasing spate of violence in the country.

In dealing with the theme we highlighted several critical areas such as:

- Health especially the HIV/AIDS scourge.
- The violation of the rights of children
- Violence against women in its many, manifestations e.g.

  Trokosi.

  Female Genital Mutilation

  Witchcraft and Widowhood Rites
  We acknowledge that violence is sometimes rooted in our scriptures as a result of the misinterpretation and misuse of scripture. In the same vein supposedly negative aspects of the traditional religion and culture are used in contemporary occultism in Ghana.

In the light of this, we propose that:

* There should be a re-examination, re-reading and re-interpretation of the scriptures and a re-evaluation of the cultural practices.

* Religious bodies such as the churches and the mosques should open crisis centers where all those who have been violated especially women, can take refuge and seek counselling.

* Religious bodies should sponsor community based programmes, especially at the grassroots to raise awareness and sensitize all on issues of violence, their manifestation and channels of help. FIDA, Legal AID and other groups may be invited to help.

* Counselling services to be opened by concerned groups to help women either by the telephone or through the post. The hotline should be made known to the public through the different channels such as Womens' Fellowship and Sponsored programmes on the radio and television.

As people of faith we believe that there are resources in the scriptures and in African Traditional Culture, which promote peace and abhor violence. Consequently we propose that.

* The sayings, proverbs, and symbols in our traditions which promote peace should be highlighted and imparted to all.

* We should create respectful relations, that will reflect the dignity and nobility of all human beings as created by God.

* We should build bridges of peace with justice in the homes and institutions both religious and secular.

* People of faith should use dialogue or negotiation as the basis for creating peace.

* Embark on intensive educational programmes on peace building in the family and in other institutions.

We also advocate that in view of the state-instituted sanctions on violence against women not being severe enough, the judiciary and the legislative organs of the State review the penalties and make them stiffer to deter people from committing acts of violence.

APPENDIX III

PUBLICITY REPORT ON THE INAUGURATION OF THE INSTITUTE OF AFRICAN WOMEN IN RELIGION AND CULTURE AT TRINITY THEOLOGICAL COLLEGE, LEGON

G.B.K. Owusu

Introduction

On March 3, 1999 the Rev. Dr. A. A. Akrong, a research fellow of the Institute of African Studies, University of Ghana, Legon tasked me to publicize the inauguration of the Institute of African Women in Religion and Culture scheduled for March 13 at the Trinity Theological College, Legon.

The publicity was phased into two:

To create sufficient media awareness before the inauguration and
To give publicity locally and internationally to the inauguration.

PRE-INAUGURATION PUBLICITY

A press release was prepared and distributed to the following media houses: Managing Director of Real Media Consultant. Accra.

a. *Electronic*

- GBC Radio New (English, Akan, Ga, Ewe, Dagbani and Nzema)
- GBC Open Door (Religious programme)
- Radio choice
- Radio Gold
- BBC African Service

b. *Print*

- Daily Graphic
- Ghanaian Times
- Weekly Spectator

- The Statesman
- Ghanaian Chronicle
- Free Press
- Crusading Guide
- The Standard
- The Independent
- The Voice

Wire Service

- Ghana New Agency
- All Africa New Agency

The release was widely used (See, attached clippings).

Inauguration

- TV3
- GTV – could not honor due to over booking
- GBC Radio News
- GBC Open Door
- Joy FM
- Radio Gold
- Daily Graphic

Ghanaian Times

- Weekly Spectator
- The Statesman

- The Independent
- The Standard
- Christian Messenger
- Free Press
- Financial Times
- Crusading Guide
- Ghana News Agency

Remarks

The overall publicity was successful. TV3, GBC – Radio and GNA which are on internet sent the stories to BBC, Reuters, Voice of Germany and CNN.

I suggest that the publicity must be sustained through feature articles, news releases, interviews, seminars, debates etc.

BUILDING FUND

Come, Build "Talitha Qumi" Centre

Talitha Qumi Centre is an institution created by Trinity Theological Seminary. It has been established to facilitate seminars with outreach programs dealing with issues of mission, humanization, and development. The center is called "Talitha, Qumi Centre" as it is our dream that African women will arise and claim the human dignity due to them as children of God, created in God's image.

The work of the Institute is an expression of hope that religion would be truly a humanizing factor in human community and in the lives of individuals.

Talitha 'Qumi Centre has a three dimensional approach to its mission.

*A Gender Sensitivity program which has been in progress since 1999 conducts seminars and conferences around Ghana and a bi-ennial African conference.

*The Centre hosts individuals, interested in studying Culture and Religion in Ghana and other African countries.

*The Centre promotes research into women's lives in the area of Culture and Religion.

During the first 4 years the Centre has been housed at the women's hostel of Trinity Theological Seminary, which has provided 2 rooms for use by the present staff.

The vision/dream of the Centre is to develop a modest conference center, as part of the Seminary.

The plan of the building is based on the Ankh, the Egyptian symbol of life. The symbol became the representation of the female in biological sciences and is now the global symbol for Woman. The building also reflects the shape of the traditional Ghanaian fertility doll, which is now a very popular artifact called Akuaba. Therefore, the centre symbolizes the vision of life-enhancement, utilizing African concepts.

The centre has a round plenary hall where people from East, West, North and South could come together to think together about the issues of life in community.

APPENDIX IV
TALITHA, QUMI CENTRE
TRINITY THEOLOGICAL SEMINARY
LEGON-GHANA

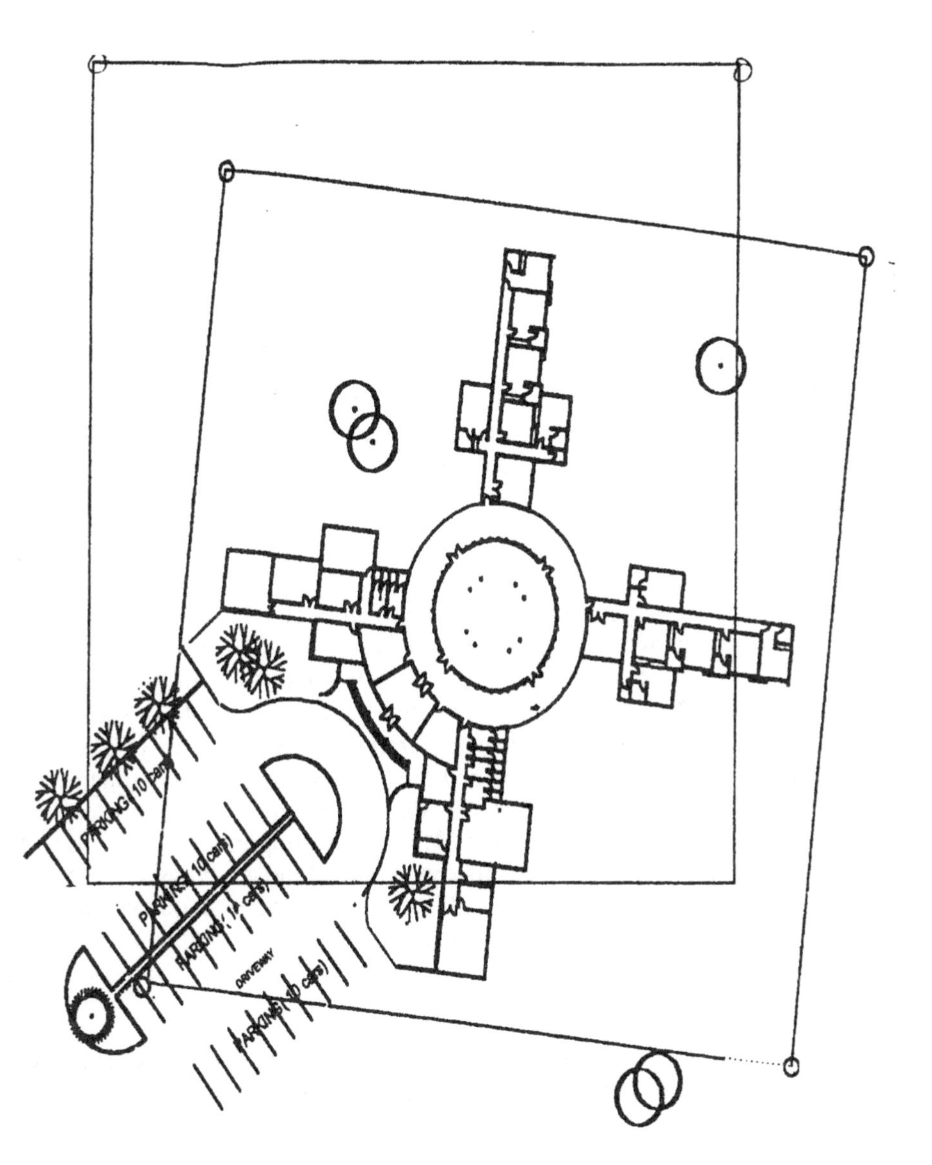

It would be a place to manifest women's global solidarity. This is the head. The rest of the body includes rooms for seminars, offices, 10 guest rooms, with double beds, a library, resource centre, and store, to allow us to offer services for retreats and guests at all times.

The Centre will need US $500,000.00 to allow us to fully construct and furnish the building.

Models of participation in the building process:

Naming Our Mothers

Name a significant woman in your life with a few lines telling us about her. She is a woman whose name must not be lost to posterity. The fundraising is based on the certainty that there must be more than a million women in living memory, whose sacrifice must be celebrated. Women whose impact we fell but whom we have not yet acknowledged. Donate towards a vision they would be proud to be associated with. The names will be complied and put into a book, surveying the empowering image of women. Each contributor is to determine the amount of the donation they wish to offer as they pay respect to their "mothers".

Women in Mission

The centre is also to honor thousands of women who have been in mission in Africa. The spread of Christianity in Africa has involved women since Empress Theodora sent a mission into the Nile Valley in the third century. During the modern period (from 18th century to present), the story is told in such a way that women are invisible. Mission cemeteries tell a different story. The brave men from Europe, North America and the Caribbeans were accompanied by courageous women, their spouses, as well as women in mission as teachers, nurses and women's work animators. There were sons and daughters as well. All these women who labored in mission to spread the good news of the risen Christ must not be forgotten. Re-call our stories to nourish our vision of an inclusive community and life-sustaining partnership.

Dedication of rooms

People may choose to sponsor the construction of one of the rooms, which will be dedicated to them in honor of their support of the Centre.

These include:

- The Hall
- A guest room
- Offices
- Library
- Resource centre
- Store

General fund raising during conferences: A donation in kind may be offered to cover the cost of a specific structure of the building; i.e. a pillar, a door, etc.

Purchasing of furnishings: Donations may be made to provide furnishing for various rooms such as

- The Hall, which will accommodate 100 people. The centre is interested in trapezium shaped tables with chairs, which will allow us all to meet together in a circle symbolizing equal participation.
- The outer corridor will also need chairs and tables for small discussion groups.
- Seminar rooms (2) will utilize similar furniture.
- Guest rooms, which are self-contained with a shower and sink and w/c, will need beds, desks and chairs. There are 10 guest rooms.
- Common rooms for the guest wings will also need tables and chairs.
- Offices (2) will need basic office equipment
- Caretaker's room
- Store

Please contact us regarding the room, which you would like to help furnish that we might provide further details.

Banking address: Women Religion and Culture/Trinity College.

FE/A 8701-5265-421-00

Submitted by: The Director,
The Institute of African Women in Religion and Culture
Trinity Theological Seminary

NAMING OUR MOTHERS

Contribute Five Thousand Cedis or more to remember a woman whose name must not be lost to posterity. There must be more than A MILLION WOMEN in LIVING MEMORY; women whose sacrifice must be celebrated. Women whose impact we feel but whom we have not yet acknowledged.

Donate Five Thousand Cedis or more per name towards a course they will be proud to associate with. It is a cause to highlight the wisdom of our mothers, queens, spouses, daughters, healers, traders, women who founded clans, villages, markets, churches and associations; women who have mothered this country and continue to carry its churches and other institutions on their backs.

These women are the inspiration behind the Institute of African Women in Religion and Culture, Trinity Theological College, Legon. The Institute will undertake women-centered studies, research and public service to throw light on and to continue the works of our fore-mothers.

BUILD TALITHA QUMI CENTRE AT TRINITY

SPONSORSHIP FORM

1. NAME OF MOTHER BEING SPONSORED......... ....
2. DATE AND PLACE OF BIRTH...
3. REASON(S) FOR YOUR CHOICE...
   ....
   ....
4. NAME OF SPONSOR..
5. SPONSOR'S ADDRESS...
   ....
6. CONTRIBUTION/DONATION US$/ / Eu/¢...
7. CHEQUE PAYABLE TO INSTITUTE OF WOMEN IN RELIGION AND CULTURE.
   Standard Chartered Bank, Legon. CEDI: A/C NO. 010-00-75698-01
   FOREIGN A/C NO. 032-15-75698-01
8. Please Mail Your Completed form and Donation to:
   THE DIRECTOR, INSTITUTE OF WOMEN IN RELIGION AND CULTURE
   TRINITY THEOLOGICAL COLLEGE
   P. O. BOX 48 LEGON
   ACCRA-GHANA.

Thank You For Your Kind Gesture.

WOMEN IN MISSION

BUILDING TALITHA QUMI CENTRE TO HONOUR

THOUSANDS OF WOMEN IN MISSION

The spread of Christianity in Africa has involved women since Empress Theodora sent a mission into the Nile Valley in the third century. During the modern period (from 18th century to present), the story is told in such a way that women are invisible. Mission cemeteries tell a different story. The brave men from Europe, North America and the Caribbean were accompanied by courageous women, their spouses as well as women in mission as teachers, nurses and "women's work" animators. There were sons and daughters as well. All these women who laboured in mission to spread the good news of the risen Christ must not be forgotten.

Re-call their stories to nourish our vision of an inclusive community and life-sustaining partnership. Talitha Qumi Centre is being raised in memory to house the Institute of African Women in Religion and Culture at the Trinity Theological College, Legon, Ghana. The Institute will facilitate the training of African Women in Religion and Culture. Send us a name(s) of a woman missionary and the means of building an ecumenical centre dedicated to these faithful women of God. End the invisibility of our sister missionaries/pioneers.

Build in memory of her!

BRING A BRICK OR A BOOK TO LAY A FOUNDATION "IN MEMORY OF HER"

BUILD TALITHA QUMI CENTRE AT TRINITY

SPONSORSHIP FORM

1. NAME OF MOTHER BEING SPONSORED....................................
2. DATE AND PLACE OF BIRTH..
3. REASON(S) FOR YOUR CHOICE..

....

....

4. NAME OF SPONSOR..
5. SPONSOR'S ADDRESS..

....

6.CONTRIBUTION/DONATION US$/ / Eu/¢......................................

7. CHEQUE PAYABLE TO INSTITUTE OF WOMEN IN RELIGION AND CULTURE.
   Standard Chartered Bank, Legon. CEDI: A/C NO. 010-00-75698-01
   FOREIGN A/C NO. 032-15-75698-01

8. Please Mail Your Completed form and Donation to:
   THE DRECTOR, INSTITUTE OF WOMEN IN RELIGION AND CULTURE TRINITY THEOLOGICAL COLLEGE

Thank You For Your Kind Gesture.

APPENDIX V
THE INSTITUTE'S BROCHURE

REACHING OUT

The Institute is open to collaboration with similar-interest groups and will seek such networking.

COMMUNICATION

For further information please

Contact:

Mercy Amba Oduyoye
The Director
INSTITUTE OF WOMEN IN RELIGION AND CULTURE
TRINITY THEOLOGICAL COLLEGE
P. O. BOX 48
LEGON, GHANA.

TEL: +233-+21-510-297
FAX: +233-+21-510-297
E-MAIL: talitha@ghana.com

CIRCLE OF CONCERNED AFRICAN WOMEN THEOLOGIANS

TRINITY THEOLOGICAL COLLEGE
LEGON GHANA
IN HOC SIGNO VINCE

INFORMATION BROCHURE

INSTITUTE OF WOMEN IN RELIGION AND CULTURE

A Project of
Trinity Theological College

CIRCLE OF CONCERNED AFRICAN WOMEN THEOLOGIANS

From 1999, Trinity Theological College will begin a pilot project of its vision to create a center for Human Development in Mission and Ministry. This project has been made possible by the aim of The Circle of Concerned African Women Theologians (The Circle) to promote women's studies in Religion and Culture in theological institutions in Africa and gender-sensitivity in Religious bodies. Ford Foundation is sponsoring this inaugural year, but we hope that with such a great challenge before us we can begin to locate sources of funding including self-supporting and low - budget event.

PROJECT DESCRIPTION

The project concentrates on women-centered studies in Religion and Culture. It will reach out to students and faculty of departments of Religion, Seminaries and Theological Colleges in Ghana. Its programs are open to all faith communities and the general public. Africa-wide links are through The Circle. The objective is to promote gender-sensitivity and gender justice especially in religion and culture.

It will promote research and publication on critical public issues related to religion and culture and seek action for transformation of attitudes and practices.

The project aims at making muted voices available and throwing light on the margins of society where some are consigned for life and for cultural and religious reasons. The aim is to establish religion as a part of life-enchancing factor in women's lives.

It is envisaged that with focus on women, Religion and gender in church and society, it will help examine religous practices and distill African culture for its enduring humanizing elements.

All events are in 1999.

March

Inauguration of the Institute at Trinity Theological College Legon: with the Theme "Women, Religion and Culture in Ghana".

March-October

Regional seminares on "Women and Religion - The Way Forward" "The Way Forward" seminars will be located at Tamale, Kumasi, Peki and Cape Coast.

Dates will be announced.

October

International Convocation:
"women and the meaning of Jubilee".

Appendix VI

Schedule of Events
From 2002 to 2005

***January - February**
Focus Groups Retreat

***March-September**
Way forward Seminars

***August-October**
Biennial Conferences
National and Pan African

***November-December**
Focus Groups Retreats

(Dates and Subjects are provided annually)

Editorial:- The Institute acknowledges with thanks the continued support of Ford Foundation and the many Ghanaian Volunteers who make these programmes possible.

Appendix VII

Members of The Advisory Board

Names

1. Dr. Rabiatu Ammah
2. Dr. Musimbi Kayoro
3. Rev. Lorene Nyarko
4. Dr. Elizabeth Amoah
5. Rev. Dinah Abbey-Mensah
6. Ms. Esther Ofei-Aboagye
7. Dr. Irene Odotei
8. Rev. Dr. Dan Antwi
9. Rev. Dr. A. A. Akrong
10. Prof. Sam Addo
11. Prof. Emmanuel A. Obeng
12. Mr. Kwesi Sam-Woode
13. Fr. Paul K. Bekye
14. Rev. Lily Oteng-Yeboah (Ex Officio-President Trinity Theological Seminary)
15. President of the Seminary: Rev. Dr. Emmanuel Asante
16. Finance Officer of the Seminary: Mr. J. A. Addy
17. Director of the Institute: Mrs. Mercy Amba Oduyoye